How to find what you need in *The Little Penguin Handbook*

If you want a quick overview of what's in this book, then you can look at the **Brief Contents** to the left.

If you see a chapter that interests you in this Brief Contents, then you can go to the page number listed or turn to the appropriate **Part opening page** for a detailed list of the contents of that part of the book.

If you want to know more about what's in a particular chapter or part, then turn to the **detailed table of contents** inside the back cover.

If you want to know where to find help for a specific issue or if you need to look up a particular term, go to the **Index** on page 265.

If you need help starting your research paper, refer to **"Research Map: Conducting Research"** at the beginning of Part 2.

If you need help with the documentation process for MLA style, refer to **"MLA Documentation Map"** at the beginning of Chapter 14.

If you need help with APA documentation, refer to the **"APA Documentation Map"** at the beginning of Chapter 15.

If you want information about CMS or CSE **documentation styles for research writing**, turn to the appropriate chapter in Part 3. You will find a complete index of sample citations for each documentation style.

You will also find **more help** at the back of this book:

- A **Glossary** with basic grammatical and usage terms, on page 255.
- A **Revision Guide** of editing and proofreading symbols
- A list of **Common Errors** of grammar, punctuation, and mechanics that many writers make

THE LITTLE PENGUIN HANDBOOK

FOURTH EDITION

LESTER FAIGLEY

University of Texas at Austin

Boston Columbus Indianapolis New York San Francisco Upper Saddle River
Amsterdam Cape Town Dubai London Madrid Milan Munich Paris Montréal Toronto
Delhi Mexico City São Paulo Sydney Hong Kong Seoul Singapore Taipei Tokyo

Editorial Director: Joseph Opiela
Senior Development Editor: Marion Castellucci
Executive Marketing Manager: Roxanne McCarley
Senior Supplements Editor: Donna Campion
Senior Media Producer: Stefanie Snajder
Digital Editor: Sara Gordus
Project Manager: Shannon Kobran
Project Coordination, Text Design, and Electronic Page Makeup: Cenveo® Publisher Services
Design Lead: Beth Paquin
Cover Images (clockwise from top left): Izabela Habur/Getty Images; Arek Malang/Shutterstock; Yuri Arcurs/Getty Images; Sturti/E+/Getty Images.
Senior Manufacturing Buyer: Roy L. Pickering, Jr.
Printer/Binder: R.R. Donnelley/Crawfordsville
Cover Printer: Lehigh-Phoenix Color/Hagerstown

Credits and acknowledgments borrowed from other sources and reproduced, with permission, in this textbook appear on page 280.

Library of Congress Cataloging-in-Publication Data

Faigley, Lester, Date-
The Little Penguin handbook / Lester Faigley, University of Texas at Austin. -- Fourth Edition.
pages cm.
Includes bibliographical references and index.
ISBN 978-0-321-94556-3
1. English language--Rhetoric--Handbooks, manuals, etc. 2. English language--Grammar--Handbooks, manuals, etc. 3. Report writing--Handbooks, manuals, etc. I. Title.
PE1408.F245 2015
808'.042--dc23
2014012801

2 3 4 5 6 7 8 9 10—DOC—17 16 15

www.pearsonhighered.com

ISBN-10: 0-321-94556-5
ISBN-13: 978-0-321-94556-3

Preface

Students learn best when they can find the right information without being overwhelmed with detail; thus *The Little Penguin Handbook* delivers the key content of a much larger book in a pocket size. Many thousands of students have become better writers with the help of *The Little Penguin Handbook.*

What's New in This Edition?

- Expanded treatment of **note taking, quoting, summarizing, and paraphrasing sources** helps writers integrate sources more effectively and avoid plagiarism (Chapters 12 and 13).
- **MLA, APA, CMS, and CSE citation examples** now include ebooks and social media posts as well as the latest style updates (Chapters 14–17).
- A new **APA documentation map** gives an overview of citing and documenting sources in APA style and shows where APA information can be found (Chapter 15).
- A new **APA style research paper** shows how to use a wide variety of sources in the body of a paper and References list (Chapter 15).
- A new chapter on **writing in online genres** highlights key considerations when composing blogs, discussion posts, and multimedia projects (Chapter 7).
- A new section on **writing case studies** provides composing guidance and an example of an academic genre commonly used in the social sciences, education, and business (Section 6b).
- New **Quick Takes** provide an at-a-glance preview of each chapter's contents, making locating information easier than ever.

MyWritingLab: Now Available for Composition

MyWritingLab is an online homework, tutorial, and assessment program that provides engaging experiences for today's instructors and students.

Visit www.mywritinglab.com for more information.

Acknowledgments

I am grateful to have worked with the best, starting with my editor, Joseph Opiela, who has had a hand in all the books I've written for Pearson. Development editor Marion Castellucci has been a joy to have as a collaborator on this edition, much valued for her knowledge, experience, and good humor. Project manager Shannon Kobran oversaw this edition and made her own contributions. Lois Lombardo at Cenveo skillfully guided the manuscript into production. Finally, I once again appreciate having the splendid Elsa van Bergen as my copy editor.

I am fortunate to have an expert group of reviewers, who were not only perceptive in their suggestions but could imagine a handbook that breaks new ground. They are Teresa Aggen, Pikes Peak Community College; Douglas Atkins, University of Kansas; Kate Berger, St. Louis Community College; Crystal Bickford, Southern New Hampshire University; Candace Boeck, San Diego State University; Jon Brammer, Three Rivers Community College; Shanti Bruce, Nova Southeastern University; Maria Cahill, Edison College–Fort Myers; Sherry Cisler, Arizona State University; Janet Dean, Bryant University; Lynee Lewis Gaillet, Georgia State University; Kami Hancock, Saint Louis University; Katherine D. Harris, San Jose State University; Brian Hays, Westmoreland County Community College; Michael Hricik, Westmoreland County Community College; Krista Hiser, Kapiolani Community College; Jeffrey Janssens, North Central State College; Marshall W. Kitchens, Oakland University; Melinda A. Knight, Montclair State University; Ellen Olmstead, Montgomery College; Shelley Palmer, Rowan-Cabarrus Community College; Martha J. Payne, Ball State University; Helen Raica-Klotz, Saginaw Valley State University; Dawn Penich-Thacker, South Mountain Community College; Carole Raybourn, Georgia Perimeter College; Melissa Reddish, Wor-Wic Community College; Alison Reynolds, University of Florida; Lynn Shaffer, Maysville Community & Technical College; David Sharpe, Ohio University; Michele Singletary, Nashville State Community College; Ginny Skinner-Linnenberg, Nazareth College; Pamela Solberg, Western Technical College; Grace M. Urbanski, Marquette University; Leah Zuidema, Dordt College.

As always, my greatest debt of gratitude is to my wife, Linda, who makes it all possible.

Lester Faigley

PART 1

Composing

1 Think as a Writer

QUICK*TAKE*

- Understand the process of communication (see below)
- Know how to get readers to take you seriously (see p. 3)

1a Think About the Process of Communication

The process of communication involves the interaction of three essential elements: the writer or speaker, the audience, and the subject. These three elements are often represented by a triangle.

Speaker, subject, and audience are each necessary for an act of communication to occur. These three elements interact with each other. Speakers make adjustments to their presentations of a subject depending on the audience (think of how you talk to small children). Just as speakers adjust to audiences, audiences continually adjust to speakers (think of how your attitude toward speakers changes when they are able to laugh at themselves).

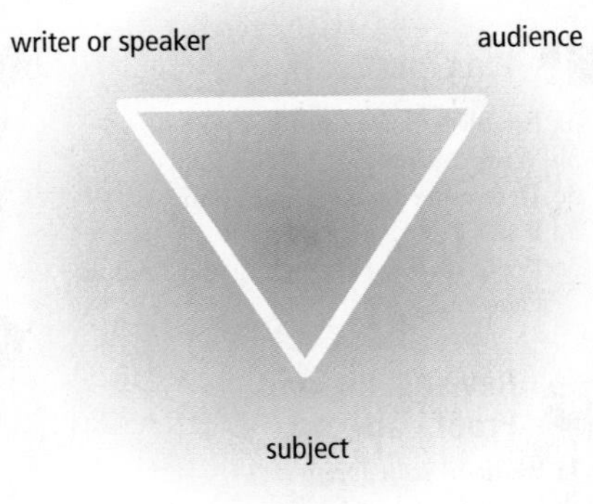

The rhetorical triangle

Think About Your Audience

In college writing, you often write for readers you know directly, including your classmates and your teachers. In the workplace, you may not always know who is going to read your reports or memos. Ask yourself who will read your writing and think about what kind of information you need to provide to engage them.

WRITING SMART

Understand your audience

- Who is most likely to read what you write?
- How much does your audience know about your subject? Are there any key terms or concepts that you will need to explain?
- How interested is your audience likely to be? If they lack interest in your subject, how can you get them engaged?
- What is their attitude likely to be toward your subject? If they hold attitudes different from yours, how can you get them to consider your views?
- What would motivate your audience to want to read what you write?

1c Think About Your Credibility

Some writers have credibility because of their standing in a given field. Most writers, however, have to convince their readers to keep reading by demonstrating knowledge of their subject and concern with their readers' needs.

WRITING SMART

Build your credibility

- How can you convince your audience that you are knowledgeable about your subject? Do you need to do research?
- How can you convince your audience that you have their interests in mind?
- What strategies can you use to enhance your credibility? Should you cite experts on your subject? Can you acknowledge opposing positions, indicating that you've taken a balanced view of your subject?
- Does the appearance, accuracy, and clarity of your writing give you credibility?

2 Read and View with a Critical Eye

QUICK*TAKE*

- Ask questions while you read (see below)
- Analyze visual texts (see p. 5)

2a Become a Critical Reader

You can become a more effective critical reader if you have a set of strategies and use them while you read.

Preview

No subject is ever completely new; it is likely that many people have talked about the subject before. Begin by asking the following questions.

- Who wrote this material?
- Where did it first appear? In a book, newspaper, magazine, or online?
- What is the topic or issue?
- Where does the writer stand on the topic or issue?
- What else has been written about the topic or issue?
- Why was it written?

Summarize

Make sure you understand exactly what is at issue. Circle any words or references that you don't know and look them up. Ask yourself

- What is the writer's main claim or question?
- If I do not find a specific claim, what is the main focus?
- What are the key ideas or concepts that the writer considers?
- What are the key terms? How does the writer define those terms?

Respond

As you read, write down your thoughts. Ask these questions.

- To what points made by the writer should I respond?
- What ideas might be developed or interpreted differently?
- What do I need to look up?

Analyze

On your second reading, analyze the structure using the following questions.

- How is the piece of writing organized?
- What does the writer assume the readers know and believe?
- Where is the evidence? Can you think of contradictory evidence?
- Does the writer acknowledge opposing views? Does the writer deal fairly with opposing views?
- What kinds of sources are cited? Are they thoroughly documented?
- How does the writer represent herself or himself?

2b Become a Critical Viewer

Like critical reading, critical viewing requires you to reflect in depth on what you see. Use the following strategies.

Preview

Critical viewing requires thinking about the context first.

- Who created this image?
- Why was it created?
- Where and when did it first appear?
- What media were used?
- What has been written about the creator or the image?

Respond

Make notes as you view the image with these questions in mind.

- What was my first impression of the image?
- After thinking more—perhaps reading more—about it, how have I changed or expanded my first impression?

Analyze

The following analytical questions apply primarily to still images.

- How is the image composed or framed?
- Where do my eyes go first?
- How does the image appeal to the values of the audience?
- Was it intended to serve a purpose besides art or entertainment?

The billboard suggests that this photograph was taken when travel by train was still popular. In fact, it was taken in 1937 by Dorothea Lange (1895–1965), who gave it the title *Toward Los Angeles, California*. The lines of the shoulder of the road, the highway, and the telephone poles slope toward a vanishing point on the horizon, giving a sense of great distance. The two figures in dark clothing walking away contrast with a rectangular billboard with a white background and white frame.

Another approach to critical viewing is to analyze the purpose of the content. In 1937 the United States was in the midst of the Great Depression and a severe drought, which forced many small farmers in middle America to abandon their homes and go to California in search of work. By placing the figures and the billboard beside each other, Lange is able to make an ironic commentary on the lives of well-off and poor Americans during the Depression.

Dorothea Lange, *Toward Los Angeles, California*.

3 Plan and Draft

QUICK*TAKE*

- Write a working thesis (see below)
- Plan a strategy (see p. 8)

3a Establish Goals and Find a Topic

Often an assignment will contain key words such as *analyze, define, describe, evaluate,* or *propose* that will guide you.

- **Analyze:** Find connections among a set of facts, events, or readings.
- **Define:** Make a claim about what something means.
- **Describe:** Observe carefully and select details.
- **Evaluate:** Argue that something is good, bad, best, or worst, according to criteria that you set out.
- **Propose:** Identify a particular problem and explain why your solution is the best one.

3b Write a Working Thesis

Having a specific focus is the key to writing a strong essay.

Use questions to focus a broad topic

Childhood obesity might be a current and interesting research topic, but it is too broad. Ask questions that will break a big topic into smaller topics.

- Why are children today more obese than children of past generations?
- How has the American food industry contributed to obesity?
- What changes in American culture have contributed to obesity?
- What strategies are effective for preventing childhood obesity?

Consider other angles to expand a narrow topic

Sometimes a topic can become too narrow or limiting. Although candy consumption may be one contributing factor leading to obesity, this narrow focus overlooks other factors that together lead to childhood obesity.

- Why do some children eat large amounts of candy yet maintain a healthy weight?
- Children have always eaten candy. Why are children today more obese than children of past generations?
- Even when parents keep kids away from candy, some still gain weight. Why?

Turn your topic into a thesis statement

Your thesis states your main idea. Much of the writing that you will do in college and in your career will have an explicit thesis, usually stated near the beginning. Your thesis should be closely tied to your purpose—to reflect on your own experience, to explain some aspect of your topic, or to argue for a position or course of action.

A reflective thesis

Watching my younger sister's struggles with her weight has taught me that childhood obesity has long-lasting psychological effects.

An informative thesis

Childhood obesity has continued to increase over the past decade despite increasing awareness of its detrimental effects.

A persuasive thesis

Parents must encourage healthy eating and exercise habits in order to reverse the growing trend toward obesity in children.

3c Determine Your Organization

Working outlines

A working outline is an initial sketch of how you will arrange the major sections of your essay or report. Jotting down main points and a few subpoints before you begin can be a great help while you are writing.

Formal outlines

A formal outline typically begins with the thesis statement, which anchors the entire outline. Each numbered or lettered item clearly supports the thesis, and the relationship among the items is clear from the outline hierarchy. Roman numerals indicate the highest level; next come capital letters, then Arabic numbers, and finally lowercase letters. The rule to remember when deciding whether you need to use the next level down is that each level must have at least two items: a "1." needs a "2."; an "a." needs a "b." Formal outlines can be helpful because they force you to look carefully at your organization.

3d Focus Your Paragraphs

Often writers will begin a paragraph with one idea, and then other ideas will occur to them while they are writing. Paragraphs confuse readers when they go in different directions. When you revise your paragraphs, check for focus.

Topic sentences

Topic sentences alert readers to the focus of a paragraph and help writers stay on topic. Topic sentences should explain the focus of the paragraph and situate it in the larger argument. Topic sentences, however, do not have to begin paragraphs, and they need not be just one sentence.

3e Write Effective Beginning and Ending Paragraphs

Effective beginning paragraphs convince the reader to read on. They capture the reader's interest and set the tone for the piece.

Start beginning paragraphs with a bang

Try beginning with one of the following strategies to get your reader's attention.

A concisely stated thesis

> If the governments of China and Russia don't soon act decisively, snow leopards will be extinct in a few years.

Images

Tons of animal pelts and bones sit in storage at Royal Chitwan National Park in Nepal. The mounds of poached animal parts confiscated by forest rangers reach almost to the ceiling. The air is stifling, the stench stomach-churning.

A problem

Ecologists worry that the construction of a natural gas pipeline in Russia's Ukok Plateau will destroy the habitat of endangered snow leopards, argali mountain sheep, and steppe eagles.

Conclude with strength

Use the ending paragraph to touch on your key points, but do not merely summarize. Leave your readers with something that will inspire them to continue to think about what you have written.

Issue a call to action

Although ecological problems in Russia seem distant, students like you and me can help protect the snow leopard by joining the World Wildlife Fund campaign.

Make recommendations

Russia's creditors would be wise to sign on to the World Wildlife Fund's proposal to relieve some of the country's debt in order to protect the snow leopard's habitat. After all, if Russia is going to be economically viable, it needs to be ecologically healthy.

Speculate about the future

Unless Nepali and Chinese officials devote more resources to snow leopard preservation, these beautiful animals will be gone in a few years.

4 Revise, Edit, and Proofread

QUICKTAKE

- Use strategies for rewriting (see below)
- Edit for specific goals (see p. 12)

4a Evaluate Your Draft

Use the following questions to evaluate your draft.

- Does your paper or project meet the assignment?
- Does your writing have a clear focus?
- Are your main points adequately developed?
- Can you rearrange sections or key points?
- Do you consider your readers' knowledge and points of view?
- Do you conclude emphatically?

When you finish, make a list of your goals for the revision.

4b Learn Strategies for Rewriting

1. **Keep your audience in mind.** Reread each paragraph's opening sentence and ask yourself whether the language is strong and engaging enough to keep your reader interested.
2. **Sharpen your focus wherever possible.** Revise your thesis and supporting paragraphs as needed. Check to see that your focus remains consistent throughout the essay.
3. **Check that key terms are adequately defined.** What are your key terms? Are they defined precisely enough to be meaningful?
4. **Develop where necessary.** Key points and claims may need more explanation and supporting evidence.
5. **Check links between paragraphs.** Underline the first and last sentences of each paragraph in your paper. Do these sentences together make a logical and coherent argument?
6. **Consider your title.** Be as specific as you can in your title, and, if possible, suggest your stance.

7. **Consider your introduction.** In the introduction you want to get off to a fast start and convince your reader to keep reading.
8. **Consider your conclusion.** Try to leave your reader with something interesting and provocative.

4c Edit for Specific Goals

1. **Check the connections between sentences.** If you need to signal a relationship between one sentence and the next, use a transitional word or phrase (words like *for example, furthermore, however, in contrast, next, similarly, therefore*).
2. **Check your sentences for clarity.** Read your paper aloud. If you notice that a sentence is hard to read or doesn't sound right, think about how you might rephrase it.
3. **Eliminate wordiness.** See how many words you can take out without losing the meaning (see Chapter 19).
4. **Use active verbs.** Anytime you can use a verb other than a form of *be* (*is, are, was, were*) or a verb ending in *-ing,* take advantage of the opportunity to make your style more lively (see Section 18b).
5. **Use specific and inclusive language.** As you read, stay alert for any vague words or phrases. Check to make sure that you have used inclusive language throughout (see Section 21d).

4d Proofread Carefully

1. **Know what your spelling checker can and can't do.** Spelling checkers do not catch wrong words (e.g., "to much" should be "too much"), missing endings ("three dog"), and other errors.
2. **Check for grammar and mechanics.** Nothing hurts your credibility with readers more than a text with numerous errors.

4e Review the Writing of Others

Your instructor may ask you to review your classmates' drafts.

1. **Begin with the big picture**—the questions in Section 4a about whether the project meets the assignment, and so on.
2. **Call attention to local problems last**—sentence construction, word choice, and errors.
3. **Write a letter to the writer,** summarizing your comments.

5 Write Arguments

QUICK*TAKE*

- Find an arguable topic (see below)
- Write a position argument (see p. 15)
- Write a proposal argument (see p. 18)

5a Write Position Arguments and Proposal Arguments

How you develop a written argument depends on your goals. You may want to convince your readers to change their way of thinking about an issue or perhaps get them to consider the issue from your perspective. Or you may want your readers to take some course of action based on your argument. These two kinds of arguments can be characterized as **position** and **proposal arguments**.

5b Find an Arguable Topic and Make a Claim

Position arguments often take two forms—definition arguments and rebuttal arguments.

Definition arguments. People argue about definitions (for example, is graffiti vandalism or is it art?) because of the consequences of something's being defined in a certain way. If you can get your audience to accept your definition, then usually your argument will be successful.

Definition arguments take the form shown here.

> Something is (or is not) ___________ because it has (or does not have) Criteria A, Criteria B, and Criteria C (or more).

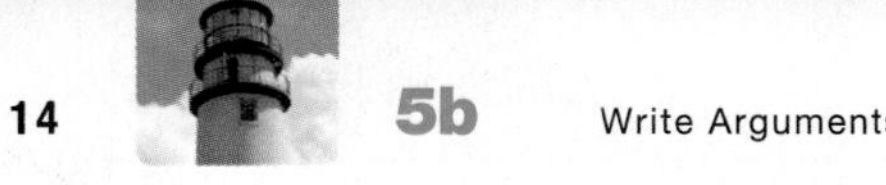

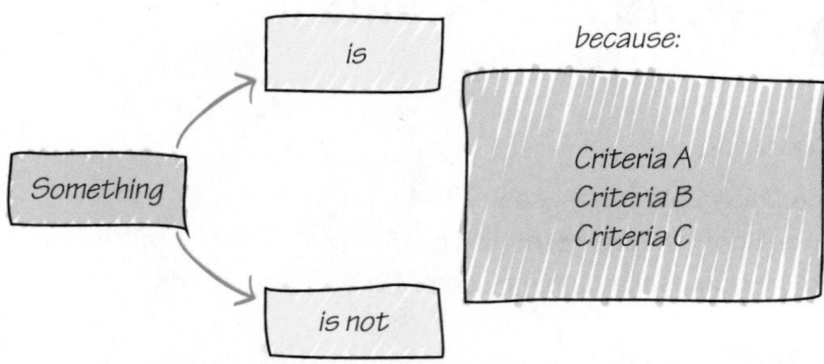

Graffiti is art because it is a means of self-expression, it shows an understanding of design principles, and it stimulates both the senses and the mind.

Rebuttal arguments take the opposite position. You can challenge the criteria a writer uses to make a definition or you can challenge the evidence that supports the claim. Often the evidence presented is incomplete or wrong. Sometimes you can find counterevidence. Often when you rebut an argument, you identify one or more fallacies in that argument.

Rebuttal arguments take this form.

The opposing argument has serious shortcomings that undermine the claim because

flawed reason 1

flawed reason 2

The great white shark gained a false reputation as a "man eater" from the 1975 movie Jaws, but in fact attacks on humans are rare and most bites have been "test bites," which is a common shark behavior with unfamiliar objects.

Supporting claims with reasons

The difference between a slogan, such as *Oppose candidate X*, and an arguable claim, such as *Oppose candidate X because she will not lower taxes and not improve schools*, is the presence of a reason linked to the claim. A reason is typically offered in a **because clause**, a statement that begins with the word *because* and provides a supporting reason for the claim. The word *because* signals a **link** between the reason and the claim.

5c Organize and Write a Position Argument

1 Before you write

Think about your readers

- What do your readers already know about the subject?
- What is their attitude toward the subject? If it is different from your position, how can you address the difference?
- What are the chances of changing the opinions and beliefs of your readers? If your readers are unlikely to be moved, can you get them to acknowledge that your position is reasonable?
- Are there any sensitive issues you should be aware of?

2 Write an introduction

Engage your readers quickly

- Get your readers' attention with an example of what is at stake.
- Define the subject or issue.
- State your thesis to announce your position.

3 Organize and write the body of your paper

Develop reasons

- Can you argue from a definition? Is ______ a ______?
  EXAMPLES
  Are cheerleaders athletes?
  Are zoos guilty of cruelty to animals?
- Can you compare and contrast? Is ______ like or unlike ______?
- Can you argue that something is good (better, bad, worse)?
- Can you argue that something caused (or may cause) something else?
- Can you refute objections to your position?

Support reasons with evidence

- Can you support your reasons by going to a site and making observations?
- Can you find facts, statistics, or statements from authorities to support your reasons?

Consider opposing views

- Acknowledge other stakeholders for the issue and consider their positions.
- Explain why your position is preferable.
- Make counter arguments if necessary.

4 Write a conclusion

End with more than a summary

- Offer further evidence in support of your thesis. Reinforce what is at stake. Give an example that gets at the heart of the issue.

5 Revise, revise, revise

Evaluate your draft

- Make sure your position argument meets the assignment requirements.
- Can you sharpen your thesis to make your position clearer?
- Can you add additional reasons to strengthen your argument?
- Can you supply additional evidence?
- When you have finished revising, edit and proofread carefully.

5d Make a Proposal

Every day we hear and read arguments that some action should be taken. We even make these arguments ourselves: We should eat better; we should exercise more; we should change our work habits. Convincing others to take action for change is always hard. Other people may not see the problem that you see, or they may not think it is important. Nevertheless, most people aren't satisfied with doing nothing about a problem that they think is important.

In a proposal argument, you present a course of action in response to a recognizable problem. The proposal says what can be done to improve the situation or change it altogether. You

- define the problem,
- propose a solution or solutions, and
- explain why the solution is feasible and will work.

Proposal arguments take the form shown here.

SOMEONE should (or should not) do SOMETHING because ______

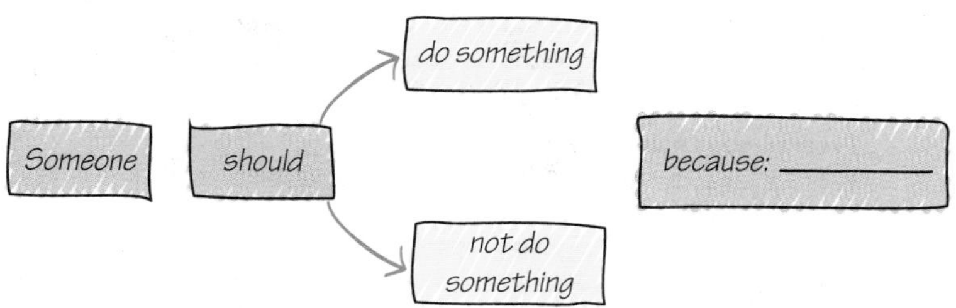

We should convert existing train tracks in the downtown areas to a light-rail system and build a new freight track around the city because we need to relieve traffic and parking congestion downtown.

5e Organize and Write a Proposal Argument

1 Before you write

Think about your readers

- How much are your readers affected by the problem you are addressing?
- Do your readers agree that the problem you are addressing is important?
- If your readers are unaware of the problem, how can you make them think that solving the problem is important?

2 Write an introduction

Identify the problem

- Do background research on what has been written about the problem and what solutions have been attempted.
- Summarize the problem for your readers and identify whose interests are at stake.
- Describe what is likely to happen if the problem isn't addressed.

3 Organize and write the body of your paper

Describe other solutions that have been proposed or attempted

- Explain why other solutions don't solve the problem or are unrealistic.

Present your solution

- Make clear the goals of your solution. Some solutions do not completely solve the problem.
- Describe the steps of your proposal in detail.
- Describe the positive consequences (or how negative consequences might be avoided) as a result of your proposal.

Argue that your solution can be done

- Your proposal is a good idea only if it can be put into practice, so explain how it is feasible.
- If your proposal requires money, explain where the money will come from.
- If your proposal requires people to change their present behavior, explain how they can be convinced to change.

4 Write a conclusion

End with a call to action

- Think about shared community values—such as fairness, justice, or clean air and water—that you might raise with your readers.
- Put your readers in the position that, if they agree with you, they will take action.
- Explain exactly what they need to do.

5 Revise, revise, revise

Evaluate your draft

- Make sure your proposal argument meets the requirements of the assignment.
- Can you better explain the problem or provide more evidence about it?
- Can you add additional evidence that your proposal will solve the problem?
- Do you explain why your solution is better than other possible solutions?
- When you have finished revising, edit and proofread carefully.

You can read an example proposal argument in Section 14k.

6 Write in Academic Genres

QUICK*TAKE*

- Write an observation (see below)
- Write a case study (see p. 22)
- Write a rhetorical analysis (see p. 24)
- Write an essay exam (see p. 26)

6a Write an Observation

Observations are common in the natural sciences and in social science disciplines such as psychology, sociology, and education. Observations should include as many relevant and specific details as possible.

Elements of an observation

Title	State the content precisely.
Description and context	Be specific about what or whom you are observing. How did you limit your site or subject? What background information do readers need?
Record of observations	Report what you observed in some logical order: chronologically, or from most obvious features to least obvious, or using some other pattern.
Conclusion or summary	Give your readers a framework in which to understand your observations. What conclusions can you draw from them? What questions are left unanswered?

What you need to do

- Bring a laptop, tablet, or paper notebook and make extensive field notes. Provide as much information as possible about the activities you observe.
- Record exactly when you arrived and left, where you were, and exactly what you saw and heard.
- Analyze your observations before you write about them. Identify patterns and organize your report according to those patterns.

Sample observation

Animal Activity in Barton Springs Pool
from 15 April to 22 April 2014

Barton Springs Pool is a 225-meter-long, natural spring-fed pool in a limestone creek bed in Austin, Texas. It is both a wildlife habitat and a busy hub of human activity. Because of the constant flow from the springs, the water temperature is constant at 68°F (20°C), allowing swimmers to use the pool year-round.

My first observation was on 15 April from 1:45 p.m. to 4 p.m. on a warm sunny day with the air temperature at 74°F (23°C). I used a mask and snorkel to observe below the water. It was remarkable how oblivious people and wildlife were of each other. While from forty to fifty-five Austinites splashed on the surface, many fish (mostly smallmouth bass with two large channel catfish on the bottom) swam below them, and large numbers of crayfish crept along the rocky portion of the pool's bottom. Eight small turtles (red-eared sliders) alternately swam at the surface and dove below near the dam at the deep end. Twelve endangered Barton Springs salamanders (*Eurycea sosorum*), ranging in color from bright orange to paler yellow, were active by the larger spring at the center of the pool.

Specific times, weather conditions, numbers of individual species, and behaviors are recorded.

At the times when humans are nearly absent, animal activity noticeably increases. From the side of the pool on 16 April (clear, 72°F; 22°C) from 7:25 p.m. until closing at 8 p.m., I observed smallmouth bass schooling near the dam and feeding on mosquitoes and mayflies.

 Write a Case Study

Case studies are used in a wide range of fields such as nursing, psychology, business, and anthropology. Rather than giving the "big picture" about phenomena, they provide a rich, detailed portrait of a specific subject.

Elements of a case study

Introduction	Explain the purpose of your study and how or why you selected your subject. Use language appropriate to your discipline and specify the boundaries of your study.
Methodology	Explain the theories or formal process that guided your observations and analysis during the study.
Observations	Describe the "case" of the subject under study by writing a narrative, utilizing interviews, research, and other data to provide as much detail and specificity as possible.
Discussion	Explain how the variables in your case might interact. Don't generalize from your case to a larger context; stay within the limits of what you have observed.
Conclusion	What does all this information add up to? What is implied, suggested, or proven by your observations? What new questions arise?
References	Using the appropriate format, cite all the outside sources you have used. (See Chapter 15 for APA documentation and Chapter 17 for CSE documentation.)

What you need to do

- Understand the specific elements of your assignment. Ask your instructor if you aren't sure about the focus, context, or structure your case study should have.
- Use careful observation and precise, detailed descriptions to provide a complex picture with a narrow focus.
- Write your observations in the form of a narrative, placing yourself in the background (avoid using *I* or *me*).
- Analyze your findings and interpret their possible meanings, but draw your conclusions from the observed facts.

Sample excerpts from a case study

Underage Drinking Prevention Programs
in the Radisson School District

INTRODUCTION

This study examines the effect of Smith and Bingham's drinking-prevention curriculum on drinking rates in the Radisson School District, 2009–2013. Prior to 2009, the Radisson School District offered no formal drinking-prevention education. In 2009, as part of a state initiative, the district proposed several underage drinking education curricula for possible adoption. This study tracks student drinking rates from 2009 to 2013 and compares the results after introduction of the curriculum to district rates prior to implementation.

Some disciplines require title pages. See page 133 for an example of an APA title page.

The introduction identifies both the problem and the particular subject of the case study.

DISCUSSION

The data from this study showed no correlation between the curriculum and student drinking rates. Drinking rates remained unchanged before, during, and after the implementation of the curriculum. Therefore, in this case, it cannot be said that Smith and Bingham's curriculum had any measurable effect on changing students' drinking behavior.

CONCLUSION

In terms of reducing student drinking, Smith and Bingham's curriculum does not appear to be any more effective than no drinking-prevention education at all. Since no measurable results were obtained, the strong administrative support for the curriculum in the school district cannot be attributed to its success.

The conclusion sums up what has been observed. Many case studies do not give definitive answers but rather raise further questions to explore.

6c Write a Rhetorical Analysis

The goal of a rhetorical analysis is to understand how a particular act of writing or speaking influenced particular people at a particular time. Writing a rhetorical analysis (also called a "critical analysis" or "textual analysis") is a paper frequently assigned in college.

Elements of a rhetorical analysis

Introduction	Begin your analysis by giving the necessary background.
The context	Explain the relationship between the piece of writing or speaking and the larger cultural and historical circumstances in which it was produced.
The text	Describe how the writer or speaker builds trustworthiness (*ethos*), appeals to the values of the audience (*pathos*), and uses intellectual reasoning (*logos*). Look at how the organization and style support the author's purpose.
Conclusion	Draw implications from your analysis.

What you need to do

- Examine the author. What is the author's purpose: to change beliefs? to inspire action? to amuse?
- Examine the audience. Who was the intended audience? What were their attitudes and beliefs?
- Examine the larger conversation. Why did this text appear at this particular time? What else was going on?
- Examine the kind of text—a speech? an essay? a letter? an editorial? an advertisement? What are the expectations of this kind of text?
- Examine the content. What is the author's main claim or idea? How is the claim or idea supported?
- Examine the language and style. Is the style formal or informal? Does the author use humor? What metaphors are used?

Sample page from a rhetorical analysis

Jackson 2

In 1851 Sojourner Truth traveled to Akron, Ohio, to attend a women's rights convention aimed at getting Ohio to add more rights for women in its state constitution. Many local men, including several ministers, attended the convention just to heckle speakers. Sojourner Truth delivered her famous "Ain't I a Woman?" speech in this intense atmosphere. In her spontaneous lecture, Truth used her own physical and intellectual credibility to make powerful emotional appeals and convincing logical claims. Her arguments redefined the word "womanhood" and made direct connections between women's rights and the abolition of slavery for an all-white audience.

The paragraph begins by analyzing the context of Sojourner Truth's speech.

In these two sentences, Jackson makes a claim about the persuasive power of Truth's speech.

When Truth begins to speak, her words display her experience and wisdom. Rather than addressing her audience as "Ladies and gentlemen," or, "Members of the convention," Truth begins this way: "Well children, when there is so much racket there must be something out of kilter" (268). By using the word "children" to address her adult, white audience, Truth draws attention to her age and wisdom and at the same time proves that she is equal to, not subservient to, these white adults. She also refers to the heated arguments between the women and men attending the convention as "so much racket," a statement that takes her out of the arguments she is witnessing and therefore makes her seem like a voice of reason in a chaotic environment.

Jackson turns to an analysis of the text, demonstrating how Truth established her relationship to her audience in the opening of her speech.

6d Write an Essay Exam

Instructors use essay exams to test your understanding of course concepts and to assess your ability to analyze ideas independently. To demonstrate these skills, you must write an essay that responds directly and fully to the question being asked.

Elements of an essay exam

Introduction	Briefly restate the question, summarizing the answer you will provide.
Body paragraphs	Each paragraph should address a major element of the question. Order them so the reader can tell how you are responding to the question. ***Example*** Of the many factors leading to the downfall of Senator Joseph McCarthy, the Army-McCarthy hearings were the most important.
Conclusion	*Briefly* restate your answer to the question, not the question itself.

What you need to do

- Make sure you understand the question. Respond with the kinds of information and analysis the question asks you to provide.
- Plan your response before you begin writing, using an outline, list, or diagram. Note how much time you have to write your response.
- Address each element of the question, providing supporting evidence.
- Relate the point of each paragraph clearly to the larger argument.
- Save a few minutes to proofread and add information where needed.

Sample essay exam

HIS 312: Early American History Describe the economic, cultural, and political variables that led to the establishment of slavery in the American South.

Amy Zhao began her response to the essay question by jotting down ideas for each of the three categories mentioned. Her outline also served as a map for the structure of her essay.

economic	*cultural*	*political*
plantation economy	*racist ideologies*	*elite leadership of southern colonies*
trade with Europe	*divide with indentured servants*	*legislature limited to large landowners*

Multiple variables in economics, culture, and politics combined to help institutionalize slavery in the American South. Most important among these variables were the plantation economy, racist ideologies, conflict among the lowest social classes, and the stranglehold of elite landowners on the legislative process.

Amy uses the key terms from the question to indicate where she is addressing that element of the question.

Economic variables arose primarily from the southern colonies' unique geographical situation. Physically isolated from the large markets of Europe but blessed with huge quantities of arable land, the region required cheap labor in order to exploit its full economic potential. Wealthy white colonists secured large tracts of land and strongly resisted any forces that pushed for the breakup of these plantations into smaller, individually owned farm holdings. The concentrated wealth and power of the plantation owners allowed them to arrange conditions to protect their land. Slavery came to be seen as the best way to maintain their power.

7 Write in Online and Multimedia Genres

QUICK*TAKE*

- Learn how to compose a blog or a discussion post (see below)
- Learn how to create a multimedia project (see p. 30)

7a Compose Blogs and Discussion Posts

Blogs assigned for courses sometimes allow students a great deal of freedom to select their subject matter, and sometimes course blogs are on an assigned topic, such as responses to the readings. Discussion board posts are often similar to blogs, but they are typically written as a response to a question or posting by the instructor.

Elements of a successful blog

Title	**Include an informative title.**
Content	Offer something new. If you don't have anything new, then point readers to the interesting writing of others.
Writing style	Engage readers with a conversational style.
Reader friendly	Revise your entry to make it more readable and to catch errors.
Participation	Invite responses.

What you need to do

- Develop a personal voice that conveys your personality.
- Remember that your blog is a conversation. You want to get responses to what you write.
- Do your homework. Let your readers know the sources of your information.
- Keep it short. If you have a lot to say about different subjects, write more than one entry.

- Add images if they are needed.
- Provide relevant links.
- Remember that informal writing is not sloppy, error-filled writing.

Sample reading blog entry

BLOG **Posted by Jillian Akbar at 4:18 p.m.** **3 comments**
October 5, 2014

Sara Macdonald's *Holy Cow* (2002)

Sara Macdonald does not begin her voyage from Australia to India with the happiest of outlooks. Laden with memories of the terrible time she had there eleven years earlier, at first she finds her only consolation in being with her boyfriend Jonathan, a fellow journalist. Macdonald confesses that her motives are more than just companionship:

> Leaving my wonderful job was the hardest thing I've ever done but perhaps I didn't do it just for love. A part of me wanted to reclaim myself, to redefine my identity, to grow up professionally, to embrace anonymity and get rid of the stalker. (17)

Macdonald's account is engaging in her insightful depiction of India. Her observations of cultural norms, such as honoring one's family in marriage, are distant but detailed and nonjudgmental. The chapter titles suggest the irreverent tone and humor of the book including "Sex, Lies and Saving Face," "Three Weddings and a Funeral," "Insane in the Membrane," "Birds of a Feather Become Extinct Together," and "Hail Mary and Good-bye God."

Macdonald's attitude toward India lightens up in the second half of the book, and I finally could relate as she suffered an Indian summer with nothing but a television and power cuts—exactly like my boyfriend's apartment in August. She offers more on the exotic imagery of India: a lotus flower growing out of slimy water, a pink ten-foot high Mary in a sari, and the "candy-colored kingdom" of the Divine Mother in Kerala (199). She includes my favorite image of all when she returns to India and is submerged in "India's Kaleidoscope of Technicolor" to feel "like Dorothy in the land of Oz" (276).

7b Create Multimedia Projects

If you decide to create a multimedia project, find out what resources are available for students on your campus. Many colleges and universities have digital media labs, which offer workshops and can provide video and audio studios, technical assistance, equipment, and software.

Oral presentation with visuals

Example project: *Encouraging more no-kill animal shelters in your city*

- **Plan:** Visit animal shelters, interview volunteers, and take photographs. Then determine the key points you want to make.
- **Produce:** Use a simple design for your slides and avoid putting much text on them. Use your own quality photographs and simple charts and graphs to emphasize the main points.
- **Deliver:** Practice in advance and pay attention to the timing of your slides. Involve your audience by inviting responses. Finish on time or earlier.

Essay with images

Example project: *Evaluation argument concerning the poor condition of parks in your city*

- **Plan:** Visit several parks, make notes, and take photographs.
- **Produce:** Write the essay. Edit your images with an image editing program and insert them in your essay with captions.
- **Edit:** Revise your eassy using the comments of classmates and your instructor.

Video production

Example project: *Proposal to create bike lanes on a busy street near your campus*

- **Plan:** Identify locations, get permission to film if necessary, and write a script.
- **Produce:** Shoot video of the street with cars and bikes competing for lanes. Interview cyclists, drivers, and local business owners about their sense of urgency of the problem and the effects of creating bike lanes.
- **Edit:** Edit with a video editing program. Export the video into a format such as QuickTime that you can put on the Web or share as a downloadable file.

PART 2 Planning Research and Finding Sources

RESEARCH MAP: CONDUCTING RESEARCH

College research writing requires that you

- determine your goals,
- find a topic,
- ask a question about that topic,
- find out what has been written about that topic,
- evaluate what has been written about that topic, and
- make a contribution to the discussion about that topic.

Here are the steps in planning research and finding sources.

1 | Plan the research project

First, analyze what you are being asked to do; go to Section 8a.

Ask a question about a topic that interests you and narrow that topic. Go to 8b.

Determine what kinds of research you will need; go to 8c.

Conduct field research if it is appropriate for your project. See strategies for

- **CONDUCTING INTERVIEWS**; go to 11b.
- **ADMINISTERING SURVEYS**; go to 11c.
- **MAKING OBSERVATIONS**; go to 11d.

2 | Draft a working thesis

Draft a working thesis. Go to 8d.

Create a working bibliography. Go to 8e.

3 | Find and track sources

Consult with a research librarian if possible, and determine where and how to start looking.

Find sources online and in print:

- for sources in **DATABASES**, go to 9b.
- for sources on the **WEB**, go to 9c.
- for **PRINT** sources, go to 9d.

Keep track of sources. Go to 9e.

4 | Evaluate sources

Decide which sources are going to be useful for your project. For each source you'll need to determine the

- **RELEVANCE** to your research question; go to 10a.

Evaluate the different types of sources you are using:

- **DATABASE** and **PRINT SOURCES**; go to 10b.
- **WEB SOURCES**; go to 10c.

8 Plan Your Research

QUICK*TAKE*

- Analyze the assignment (see below)
- Find and narrow a topic (see p. 35)
- Draft a working thesis (see p. 36)

8a Analyze the Research Task

If you have an assignment that requires research, look closely at what you are being asked to do.

Look for words that signal what is expected

- An *analysis* or *examination* asks you to look at an issue in detail, explaining its history, the people and places affected, and what is at stake.
- A *review of scholarship* requires you to summarize what key scholars and researchers have written about the issue.
- An *argument* requires you to assemble evidence in support of a claim you make.

Identify your potential readers

- How familiar are your readers with your subject?
- What background information will you need to supply?
- If your subject is controversial, what opinions or beliefs are your readers likely to hold?

Assess the project's length, scope, and requirements

- What kind of research are you being asked to do?
- What is the length of the project?
- What kinds and number of sources or field research are required?
- Which documentation style—such as MLA (see Chapter 14) or APA (see Chapter 15)—is required?

 Find and Narrow a Topic

You might begin by doing one or more of the following.

- **Visit "Research by Subject" on your library's Web site.** Clicking on a subject such as "African and African American Studies" will take you to a list of online resources. Often you can find an e-mail link to a reference librarian who can assist you.
- **Look for topics in your courses.** Browse your course notes and readings. Are there any topics you might want to explore in greater depth?
- **Consult a specialized encyclopedia.** Specialized encyclopedias focus on a single area of knowledge, go into more depth about a subject, and often include bibliographies. Check if your library database page has a link to the Gale Virtual Reference Library, which offers entries from many specialized encyclopedias and reference sources.
- **Look for topics as you read.** When you read actively, you ask questions and respond to ideas in the text. Review what you wrote in the margins or the notes you have made about something you read that interested you. You may find a potential topic.

It can be tricky to find a balance between what you want to say about a topic and the amount of space in which you have to say it. Usually your instructor will suggest a length for your project, which should help you decide how to limit your topic. If you suspect your topic is becoming unmanageable and your project may be too long, look for ways to narrow your focus.

Off track	A 5-page paper on European witch hunts
On track	A 5-page paper tracing two or three major causes of the European witch hunts of the fifteenth and sixteenth centuries
Off track	A 10-page paper on accounting fraud
On track	A 10-page paper examining how a new law would help prevent corporate accounting fraud

8c Determine What Kind of Research You Need

When you begin your research, you will have to make a few educated guesses about where to look. Ask these questions before you start.

- How much information do you need? The assignment may specify the number of sources you should consult.
- Are particular types of sources required? If so, do you understand why those sources are required?
- How current should the information be? Some assignments require you to use the most up-to-date information you can locate.

Secondary research

Most people who do research rely partly or exclusively on the work of others as sources of information. Research based on the work of others is called **secondary research**. Chapters 9 and 10 explain in detail how to find and evaluate database, Web, and print sources.

Primary research

Much of the research done at a university creates new information through **primary research**: experiments, data-gathering surveys and interviews, detailed observations, and the examination of historical documents. Chapter 11 explains how to plan and conduct three types of field research: interviews (11b), surveys (11c), and observations (11d).

8d Draft a Working Thesis

If you ask a focused and interesting research question, your answer will be your **working thesis**. This working thesis will be the focus of the remainder of your research and ultimately your research project.

Ask questions about your topic

When you have a topic that is interesting to you, manageable in scope, and possible to research using sources or doing field research, then your next task is to ask researchable questions.

Explore a definition

- While many (most) people think X is a Y, can X be better thought of as a Z?

  Most people think of deer as harmless animals that are benign to the environment, but their overpopulation devastates young trees in forests, leading to loss of habitat for birds and other species that depend on those trees.

Evaluate a person, activity, or thing

- Can you argue that a person, activity, or thing is either good, better, or best (or bad, worse, or worst) within its class?

  Fender Stratocasters from the 1950s remain the best electric guitars ever made because of their versatility, sound quality, and player-friendly features.

Examine why something happened

- Can you argue that while there were obvious causes of Y, Y would not have occurred had it not been for X?

  College students are called irresponsible when they run up high credit card debts that they cannot pay off, but these debts would not have occurred if credit card companies did not aggressively market credit cards and offer high lines of credit to students with no income.

- Can you argue for an alternative cause rather than the one many people assume?

  The defeat of the Confederate Army at the Battle of Gettysburg in July 1863 is often cited as the turning point in the Civil War, but in fact the South was running out of food, equipment, and soldiers, and it lost its only real chance of winning when Great Britain failed to intervene on its side.

Counter objections to a position

- Can the reverse or opposite of an opposing claim be argued?

New medications that relieve pain are welcomed by runners and other athletes, but these drugs also mask signals that our bodies send us, increasing the risk of serious injury.

Propose a solution to a problem

- Can you propose a solution to a local problem?

  The traffic congestion on our campus could be eased by creating bike lanes on College Drive, which would encourage more students, faculty, and staff to commute by bicycle.

Turn your answers into a working thesis

Topic	Reading disorders
Researchable question	Why do some people learn to read top-to-bottom Chinese characters more easily than left-to-right alphabetic writing?
Working thesis	The direction of text flow may be an important factor in how an individual learns to read.

 Create a Working Bibliography

When you begin to collect your sources, make sure you get full bibliographic information for everything you might want to use in your project: articles, books, Web sites, and other materials. Decide which documentation style you will use. If your instructor does not tell you which style is appropriate, ask. (The major documentation styles—MLA, APA, CMS, and CSE—are dealt with in detail in Chapters 14–17.)

Find the necessary bibliographic information

Chapter 9 gives instructions on what information you will need to collect for each kind of source. In general, as you research and develop a working bibliography, the rule of thumb is to write down more information rather than less. You can always delete unnecessary information when it comes time to format your citations according to your chosen documentation style (APA, MLA, CMS, or CSE), but it is time-consuming to go back to sources to find missing bibliographic information.

9 Find Sources

QUICK*TAKE*

- Find sources in databases (see p. 41)
- Find sources on the Web (see p. 44)
- Keep track of sources (see p. 47)

 Develop Strategies for Finding Sources

Libraries still contain many resources not available on the Web. Even more important, libraries have professional research librarians who can help you locate sources quickly.

Learn the art of effective keyword searches

Keyword searches take you to the sources you need. Start with your working thesis and generate a list of possible keywords for researching your thesis.

First, think of keyword combinations that make your search **more specific**. For example, a search for sources related to youth voter participation might focus more specifically on young adults *and*

voter registration
historical participation rates

Also think about **more general** ways to describe what you are doing—what synonyms can you think of for your existing terms? Instead of relying on "young adult," try keywords like

under 30
college students

Many databases have a thesaurus that can help you find more keywords.

WRITING SMART

Find the right kinds of sources

Type of source	Type of information	How to find them
Scholarly books	Extensive and in-depth coverage of nearly any subject	Library catalog
Scholarly journals	Reports of new knowledge and research findings by experts	Online library databases
Trade journals	Reports of information pertaining to specific industries, professions, and products	Online library databases
Popular magazines	Reports or summaries of current news, sports, fashion, entertainment subjects	Online library databases
Newspapers	Recent and current information; foreign newspapers are useful for international perspectives	Online library databases
Government publications	Government-collected statistics, studies, and reports; especially good for science and medicine	Library catalog and city, state, and federal government Web sites
Videos, audios, documentaries, maps	Information varies widely	Library catalog, Web, and online library databases

 Find Sources in Databases

Sources found through library databases have already been filtered for you by professional librarians. They will include some common sources like popular magazines and newspapers, but the greatest value of database sources are the many journals, abstracts, studies, e-books, and other writing produced by specialists whose work has been scrutinized and commented upon by other experts.

Use databases

Your library has a list of databases and indexes by subject. If you can't find this list on your library's Web site, ask a reference librarian for help. Follow these steps to find articles.

1. Select a database appropriate to your subject. (For example, if you are researching multiple sclerosis, you might start with *Health Reference Center*, *MEDLINE*, *PsycINFO*, or *PubMed*.)
2. Search the database using your list of keywords. (You could start with *multiple sclerosis* and then combine *MS* with other terms to narrow your search.)
3. Once you have chosen an article, print or e-mail to yourself the complete citation to the article. Look for the e-mail link after you click on the item you want.
4. Print or e-mail to yourself the full text if it is available. The full text is better than cutting and pasting because you might lose track of which words are yours, leading to unintended plagiarism.
5. If the full text is not available, check the online library catalog to see if your library has the journal.

WRITING SMART

Know the advantages of database versus Web sources

	Library database sources	Web sources
Speed	✓ Users can find information quickly	✓ Users can find information quickly
Accessibility	✓ Available 24/7	✓ Available 24/7
Organization	✓ Materials are organized for efficient search and retrieval	User must look in many different places for related information
Consistency and quality	✓ Librarians review and select resources	Anyone can claim to be an "expert," regardless of qualifications
Comprehen-siveness	✓ Collected sources represent a wide and representative body of knowledge	No guarantee that the full breadth of an issue will be represented
Permanence	✓ Materials remain available for many years	Materials can disappear or change in an instant
Free of overt bias	✓ Even sources with a definite agenda are required to meet certain standards of documentation and intellectual rigor	Sources are often a "soapbox" for organiza-tions or individuals with particular agendas and little knowledge or experience
Free of commercial slant	✓ Because libraries pay for their collections, sources are largely commercial-free	Sources are often motivated primarily by the desire to sell you something

Common Databases

Academic OneFile	Indexes periodicals from the arts, humanities, sciences, social sciences, and general news, with full-text articles and images.
Academic Search Premier and Complete	Provide full-text articles for thousands of scholarly publications.
ArticleFirst	Indexes journals in business, the humanities, medicine, science, and social sciences.
Business Search Premier	Provides full-text articles in all business disciplines.
EBSCOhost Research Databases	Gateway to a large collection of EBSCO databases, including *Academic Search Premier and Complete, Business Source Premier and Complete, ERIC*, and *Medline*.
General OneFile	Contains millions of full-text articles about a wide range of academic and general-interest topics.
Google Books	Allows you to search within books and gives you snippets surrounding search terms for copyrighted books. Many books out of copyright have the full text. Available for everyone.
Google Scholar	Searches scholarly literature according to criteria of relevance. Available for everyone.
JSTOR	Provides scanned copies of scholarly journals.
LexisNexis Academic	Provides full text of a wide range of newspapers, magazines, government and legal documents, and company profiles from around the world.
ProQuest Databases	Like EBSCOhost, ProQuest is a gateway to a large collection of databases with over 100 billion pages, including the best archives of doctoral dissertations and historical newspapers.

9c Find Sources on the Web

The Web offers you some resources for current topics that would be difficult or impossible to find in a library. The key to success is knowing where you are most likely to find current and accurate information about the particular question you are researching, and knowing how to access that information.

Use search engines wisely

Search engines designed for the Web work in ways similar to library databases and your library's online catalog but with one major difference. Databases typically do some screening of the items they list, but search engines potentially take you to everything on the Web—millions of pages in all.

Most search engines offer you the option of an advanced search, which gives you the opportunity to limit numbers. For example, if you want to limit a search for *multiple sclerosis* to government Web sites such as the National Institutes of Health, you can specify the domain as **.gov**.

Find online government sources

The federal government has made many of its publications available on the Web. Often the most current and most reliable statistics are government statistics. Among the more important government resources are the following.

- **Census Bureau** (www.census.gov). Contains a wealth of links to sites for population, social, economic, and political statistics, including the *Statistical Abstract of the United States* (www.census.gov/compendia/statab)
- **CIA World Factbook** (www.cia.gov/library/publications/the-world-factbook). Resource for geographic, economic, demographic, and political information on the nations of the world
- **Library of Congress** (www.loc.gov). Many resources of the largest library in the world available on the Web
- **National Institutes of Health** (www.nih.gov). Extensive health information, including MedlinePlus searches

- **NASA** (www.nasa.gov). A rich site with much information and images concerning space exploration and scientific discovery
- **Thomas** (thomas.loc.gov). The major source of legislative information, including bills, committee reports, and voting records of individual members of Congress
- **USA.gov** (www.usa.gov). The place to start when you are not sure where to look for government information

Find online reference sources

Your library's Web site may have a link to **reference sites**, either on the main page or under another heading like **research tools.**

Reference sites are usually organized by subject, and you can find resources under the subject heading.

- **Business information** (links to business databases and sites like *Hoover's* that profile companies)
- **Dictionaries** (including the *Oxford English Dictionary* and various subject dictionaries and language dictionaries)

WRITING SMART

Know the limitations of *Wikipedia*

Wikipedia is a valuable resource for current information and for popular culture topics that are not covered in traditional encyclopedias. You can find out, for example, that SpongeBob SquarePants's original name was "SpongeBoy," but it had already been copyrighted.

Nevertheless, many instructors and the scholarly community in general do not consider *Wikipedia* a reliable source of information for a research project. The fundamental problem with *Wikipedia* is stability, not whether the information is correct or incorrect. *Wikipedia* and other wikis constantly change. The underlying idea of documenting sources is that readers can consult the same sources that you consulted. To be on the safe side, treat *Wikipedia* as you would a blog. Consult other sources to confirm what you find on *Wikipedia*, and cite those sources.

- **Encyclopedias** (including *Britannica Online* and others)
- **Reference books** (commonly used books like atlases, almanacs, biographies, handbooks, and histories)

Search interactive media

Several search engines have been developed for interactive media. *Facebook* and *Twitter* also have search engines for their sites.

9d Find Print Sources

No matter how current the topic you are researching, you will likely find information in print sources that is simply not available online. Print sources have other advantages as well.

- Books are shelved according to subject, allowing easy browsing.
- Books often have bibliographies, directing you to other research on the subject.
- You can search for books in multiple ways: author, title, subject, or call letter.
- The majority of print sources have been evaluated by scholars, editors, and publishers, who decided whether they merited publication.

Find books

The floors of your library where books are shelved are referred to as *the stacks.* The call number will enable you to find the item in the stacks. You will need to consult the location guide for your library, which gives the level and section where an item is shelved.

Find journal articles

Like books, scholarly journals provide in-depth examinations of subjects. The articles in scholarly journals are written by experts, and they usually contain lists of references that can guide you to other research on a subject.

Some instructors frown on using popular magazines, but these journals can be valuable for researching current opinion on a particular topic.

Databases increasingly contain the full text of articles, allowing you to read and copy the contents onto your computer.

9e Keep Track of Sources

As you begin to collect your sources, make sure you get full bibliographic information for everything you might want to use in your project. Decide which documentation style you will use. (The major documentation styles—MLA, APA, CMS, and CSE—are dealt with in detail in Chapters 14–17.)

Locate elements of a citation in database sources

For any source you find on a database, MLA style requires you to provide the full print information, the name of the database in italics, the medium of publication (*Web*), and the date you accessed the database. If page numbers are not included, use *n. pag*. Do *not* include the URL of the database.

Author's name	Shefner, Ruth
Title of article	"Politics Deserve Teens' Attention"
Publication information	
Name of periodical	*Post-Standard* [Syracuse]
Date of publication (and edition for newspapers)	28 Nov. 2006, final ed.
Section and page number	B3
Database information	
Name of database	*LexisNexis Academic*
Date you accessed the site	28 Apr. 2014

The citation would appear as follows in an MLA-style works-cited list (see Section 14g).

Shefner, Ruth. "Politics Deserve Teens' Attention." *Post-Standard* [Syracuse] 28 Nov. 2006, final ed.: B3. *LexisNexis Academic*. Web. 28 Apr. 2014.

APA style no longer requires listing the names of common databases or listing the date of access, unless the content is likely to change (see Section 15e). If you name the database, do not list the URL.

> Shefner, R. (2006, November 28). Politics deserve teens' attention. *The Post-Standard*, p. B3. Retrieved from LexisNexis Academic database.

Locate elements of a citation in Web sources

As you conduct your online research, make sure you collect the necessary bibliographic information for everything you might want to use as a source. Because of the potential volatility of Web sources (they can and do disappear overnight), their citations require extra information. Depending on the citation format you use, you'll arrange this information in different ways.

Collect the following information about a Web site:

Author's name, if available (if not, use the associated institution or organization)	Samadzadeh, Nozlee
Title of article	"Farm Update: The Third Annual Jack Hitt Annual Last Day of Classes Pig Roast"
Publication information	
Name of site or online journal	*Yale Sustainable Food Project Student Blog*
Publisher or Sponsor of the site (for MLA style)	Yale Sustainable Food Project
Date of publication (for an article) or of site's last update	3 May 2010
Date you accessed the site	10 May 2014
URL (for some APA formats, including blogs)	http://yalesustainablefoodproject.wordpress.com/2010/05/03/farm-update-the-third-annual-jack-hitt-annual-last-day-of-classes-pig-roast/

An MLA works-cited entry for this article would look like this:

Samadzadeh, Nozlee. "Farm Update: The Third Annual Jack Hitt Annual Last Day of Classes Pig Roast." *Yale Sustainable Food Project Student Blog*. Yale Sustainable Food Project, 3 May 2010. Web. 10 May 2014.

In an APA references list, the citation would look like this:

Samadzadeh, N. (2010, May 3). Farm update: The Third Annual Jack Hitt Annual Last Day of Classes Pig Roast. Message posted to http://yalesustainablefoodproject.wordpress.com/2010/05/03/farm-update-the-third-annual-jack-hitt-annual-last-day-of-classes-pig-roast/

Locate elements of a citation in print sources

For books you will need, at minimum, the following information, which can typically be found on the front and back of the title page:

Author's name	Ojito, Mirta
Title of book	*Finding Manaña: A Memoir of a Cuban Exile*
Publication information	
Place of publication	New York
Name of publisher	Penguin
Date of publication	2005
Medium of publication	Print

Here's how the book would be cited in an MLA-style works-cited list:

Ojito, Mirta. *Finding Manaña: A Memoir of a Cuban Exile*. New York: Penguin, 2005. Print.

Here's the APA citation for the same book:

Ojito, M. (2005). *Finding manaña: A memoir of a Cuban exile*. New York, NY: Penguin.

You will also need the page numbers if you are quoting directly or referring to a specific passage, and the title and author of the individual chapter if your source is an edited book with contributions by several people.

For journals you will need the following:

Author's name	Romano, Susan
Title of article	"'Grand Convergence' in the Mexican Colonial Mundane: The Matter of Introductories"
Publication information	
Name of journal	*Rhetoric Society Quarterly*
Volume number and issue number	40.1
Date of publication (and edition for newspapers)	2010
Page numbers of the article	71–93
Medium of publication	Print
Document Object Identifier (DOI), if available, for APA	10.1080/02773940903413407

An entry in an MLA-style works-cited list would look like this:

Romano, Susan. "'Grand Convergence' in the Mexican Colonial Mundane: The Matter of Introductories." *Rhetoric Society Quarterly* 40.1 (2010): 71-93. Print.

And in APA style, like this:

Romano, S. (2010). "Grand convergence" in the Mexican colonial mundane: The matter of introductories. *Rhetoric Society Quarterly, 40,* 71–93. doi: 10.1080/02773940903413407

10 Evaluate Sources

QUICK*TAKE*

- Determine the relevance of sources (see below)
- Evaluate database and print sources (see below)
- Evaluate Web sources (see p. 52)

10a Determine the Relevance of Sources

- Does a source you have found address your research question?
- Does a source support or disagree with your working thesis? (You should not throw out work that challenges your views. Representing opposing views accurately enhances your credibility.)
- Does a source add significant information?
- Is the source current? (For most topics, try to find the most up-to-date information.)
- What indications of possible bias do you note in the source?

10b Evaluate Database and Print Sources

Printed and online materials in your library undergo review by professional librarians who select them to include in their collections. Library database collections, which your library pays to access, are also screened, which eliminates many poor-quality sources.

This initial screening doesn't free you, however, from the responsibility of evaluating the quality of the sources. Many printed and database sources contain their share of inaccurate, misleading, and biased information. Also, all sources carry the risk of being outdated when you are looking for current information.

WRITING SMART

Checklist for evaluating database and print sources

Over the years librarians have developed a set of criteria for evaluating sources, and you should apply them in your research.

1. **Source.** Who published the book or article? Enter the publisher's name on *Google* or another search engine to learn about the publisher. Scholarly books and articles in scholarly journals are generally more reliable than popular magazines and books, which tend to emphasize what is sensational or entertaining at the expense of accuracy and comprehensiveness.
2. **Author.** Who wrote the book or article? What are the author's qualifications? Enter the author's name on *Google* or another search engine to learn more about him or her. Does the author represent an organization?
3. **Timeliness.** How current is the source? If you are researching a fast-developing subject such as treating ADHD, then currency is very important, but even historical topics are subject to controversy or revision.
4. **Evidence.** Where does the evidence come from—facts, interviews, observations, surveys, or experiments? Is the evidence adequate to support the author's claims?
5. **Biases.** Can you detect particular biases of the author? How do the author's biases affect the interpretation offered?
6. **Advertising.** For print sources, is advertising a prominent part of the journal or newspaper? How might the ads affect the credibility or the biases of the information that gets printed?

10c Evaluate Web Sources

Nearly every large company and political and advocacy organization has a Web site. We expect these sites to represent the company or the point of view of the organization. Many sites on the Web, however, are not so clearly labeled.

WRITING SMART

Checklist for evaluating Web sources

Use these criteria for evaluating Web sites.

1. **Source.** What organization sponsors the Web site? Look for the site's owner at the top or bottom of the home page or in the Web address. Enter the owner's name on *Google* or another search engine to learn about the organization. If a Web site doesn't indicate ownership, then you have to make judgments about who put it up and why.
2. **Author.** Is the author identified? Look for an "About Us" link if you see no author listed. Enter the author's name on *Google* or another search engine to learn more about the author. Often Web sites give no information about their authors other than an e-mail address, if that. In such cases it is difficult or impossible to determine the author's qualifications. Be cautious about information on an anonymous site.
3. **Purpose.** Is the Web site trying to sell you something? Many Web sites are infomercials that might contain useful information, but they are no more trustworthy than other forms of advertising. Is the purpose to entertain? To inform? To persuade?
4. **Timeliness.** When was the Web site last updated? Look for a date on the home page. Many Web pages do not list when they were last updated; thus you cannot determine their currency.
5. **Evidence.** Are sources of information listed? Any factual information should be supported by indicating where the information came from. Reliable Web sites that offer information will list their sources.
6. **Biases.** Does the Web site offer a balanced point of view? Many Web sites conceal their attitude with a reasonable tone and seemingly factual evidence such as statistics. Citations and bibliographies do not ensure that a site is reliable. Look carefully at the links and sources cited, and peruse the "About Us" link if one is available.

11 Plan Field Research

QUICK*TAKE*

- Conduct informative interviews (see below)
- Design and administer surveys (see p. 55)
- Make detailed observations (see p. 56)

11a Know What You Can Obtain from Field Research

Even though much of the research you do for college courses will be secondary research conducted at a computer or in the library, some topics do call for primary research, requiring you to gather information on your own. Field research of this kind can be especially important for exploring local issues. It is also used extensively in professions that you may be joining after college.

Three types of field research that can usually be conducted in college are **interviews, surveys,** and **observations.**

- **Interviews.** Interviewing experts on your research topic can help build your knowledge base. You can use interviews to discover what the people most affected by a particular issue are thinking and feeling.
- **Surveys.** Short surveys can often provide insight on local issues.
- **Observations.** Local observation can be a valuable source of data. For example, if you are researching why a particular office on your campus does not operate efficiently, observe what happens when students enter and how they are handled by the staff.

11b Conduct Interviews

Before you contact anyone to ask for an interview, think carefully about your goals; knowing what you want to find out through your interviews will help you determine whom you need to interview and what questions you need to ask.

- Decide what you want or need to know and who best can provide that for you.
- Schedule each interview in advance, and let the person know why you are conducting the interview.
- Plan your questions in advance. Write down a few questions and have a few more in mind. Listen carefully so you can follow up on key points.
- Come prepared with a notebook, tablet, or laptop for taking notes and jotting down short quotations. Note the date, time, place, and subject of the interview. If you want to record the interview, ask for permission in advance.
- When you are finished, thank your subject and ask his or her permission to get in touch again if you have additional questions.
- When you are ready to incorporate the interview into a paper or project, think about what you want to highlight from the interview and which direct quotations to include.

11c Administer Surveys

Use surveys to find out what large groups of people think about a topic (or what they are willing to admit they think). Surveys need to be carefully designed.

- Write a few specific questions. To make sure your questions are clear, test them on a few people before you conduct the survey.
- Include one or two open-ended questions, such as "What do you like about X?" "What don't you like about X?" Open-ended questions can be difficult to interpret, but sometimes they turn up information you had not anticipated.
- Decide whom you need to survey and how many people to include. If you want to claim that the results of your survey represent the views of residents of your dormitory, your method of selecting respondents should give all residents an equal chance to be selected. Don't select only your friends.
- Decide how you will contact participants in your survey. If you are going to mail or e-mail your survey, include a statement about

what the survey is for and a deadline for returning it. You may need to get permission to conduct a survey on private property.

- Think about how you will interpret your survey. Multiple-choice formats make data easy to tabulate, but often they miss key information. Open-ended questions will require you to figure out a way to analyze responses.
- When writing about the results, be sure to include information about who participated in the survey, how the participants were selected, and when and how the survey was administered.

11d Make Observations

Simply observing what goes on in a place can be an effective research tool. Your observations can inform a controversy or topic by providing a vivid picture of real-world activity.

- Choose a place where you can observe with the least intrusion. The less people wonder about what you are doing, the better.
- Carry a notebook, tablet, or laptop and write extensive field notes. Get down as much information as you can and worry about analyzing it later.
- Record the date, exactly where you were, exactly when you arrived and left, and important details like the number of people present.

At some point you have to interpret the data. When you analyze your observations, think about what constitutes normal and unusual activities for this place. What can you determine about the purposes of these activities?

PART 3 Incorporating and Documenting Sources

12 Use Sources Effectively

QUICK*TAKE*

- Decide when to quote and when to paraphrase (see below)
- Take notes effectively (see p. 59)
- Use quotations effectively (see p. 59)
- Use summaries and paraphrases effectively (see p. 63)

Decide When to Quote and When to Summarize and Paraphrase

Use sources to support what you say; don't expect them to say it for you. Next to plagiarism, the worst mistake you can make with sources is to string together a series of long quotations. This strategy leaves your readers wondering whether you have anything to say. Relying too much on quotations from others also makes for a bumpy read. Think about how each source relates to your thesis.

When to quote and when to paraphrase

The general rule in deciding when to include direct quotations and when to paraphrase lies in the importance of the original wording.

- If you want to refer to an idea or fact and the original wording is not critical, make the point in your own words and cite the source.

  The residents of New York City, which is often imagined as an ecological nightmare, in fact use less gasoline than those of any other American city because 82% walk, bike, or take public transportation to their workplaces (Owen 2). [Here the facts are important, not the original wording.]

- Save direct quotations for language that is memorable or conveys the character of the source.

  Edward Glaesner argues that "if you love nature, stay away from it. The best means of protecting nature is to live in the heart of a city" (18). [Here the original language gives the core argument.]

12b Take Notes Effectively

The most important thing when taking notes is to take care to distinguish source words from your own words. Don't mix words from the source with your own words. Create a folder for your research project and clearly label the files.

- **Create a working bibliography and make separate files for content notes.** Create a file for each source. If you work on paper, use a separate page for each source. Also write down all the information you need for a list of works cited or a list of references in your working bibliography.
- **If you copy anything from a source when taking notes, place those words in quotation marks and note the page number(s) where those words appear.** If you copy words from an online source, take special care to note the source. You could easily copy online material and later not be able to find where it came from.
- **Print out the entire source or email to yourself so you can refer to it later.** Having print copies or complete files allows you to double-check later that you haven't used words from the source by mistake and that any words you quote are accurate.

12c Use Quotations Effectively

Effective research writing builds on the work of others. You can summarize or paraphrase the work of others, but often it is best to let authors speak in your text by quoting their exact words. Indicate the words of others by placing them inside quotation marks and giving a citation to the source.

Use quotation marks for direct quotations

Gabriella Lopez decided to include the highlighted words from the original below in her text.

Original text

Questionnaires on food attitudes and behavior were completed by 2,200 American undergraduates from 6 regionally dispersed college campuses. Results indicate that a substantial minority of women and a much smaller minority of men have major concerns about eating and food with respect to both weight and health.

Gabriella placed quotation marks around the words she took from the source. She also included an in-text citation with the authors' names so that her readers could find her source in her Works Cited and the page number where she found the words (see p. 104). Notice that the in-text citation is after the closing quotation mark but before the period.

> According to a survey of 2,200 American college students, a significant number of women and a smaller group of men "have major concerns about eating and food with respect to both weight and health" (Rozin, Bauer, and Catanese 132).

12d Integrate Quotations

All sources should be well integrated into the fabric of your project. Introduce quotations by attributing them in your text.

> Even those who fought for the United States in the U.S.-Mexican War of 1846 were skeptical of American motives: "We were sent to provoke a fight, but it was essential that Mexico should commence it" (Grant 68).

The preceding quotation is used correctly, but it loses the impact of the source. Compare it with the following.

> Many soldiers who fought for the United States in the U.S.-Mexican War of 1846 were skeptical of American motives, including Civil War hero and future president Ulysses S. Grant, who wrote: "We were sent to provoke a fight, but it was essential that Mexico should commence it" (68).

Use signal phrases

Signal verbs often indicate your stance toward a quotation. Introducing a quotation with "X says" or "X believes" tells your readers nothing. Find a livelier verb that suggests how you are using the source. For example, if you write "X contends," your reader is alerted that you likely will disagree with the source. Be as precise as possible.

Signal phrases that report information or a claim

X argues that . . .
X asserts that . . .

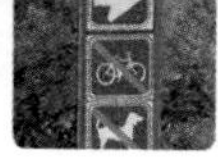

X claims that . . .
X observes that . . .
As X puts it, . . .
X reports that . . .
As X sums it up, . . .

Signal phrases when you agree with the source

X affirms that . . .
X has the insight that . . .
X points out insightfully that . . .
X theorizes that . . .
X verifies that . . .

Signal phrases when you disagree with the source

X complains that . . .
X contends that . . .
X denies that . . .
X disputes that . . .
X overlooks that . . .
X rejects that . . .
X repudiates that . . .

Signal phrases in the sciences

Signal phrases in the sciences often use the past tense, especially for interpretations and commentary.

X described . . .
X found . . .
X has suggested . . .

Introduce block quotations

Long direct quotations, called **block quotations**, are indented from the margin instead of being placed in quotation marks. In MLA style, a quotation longer than four lines should be indented 1 inch. A quotation of forty words or longer is indented ½ inch in APA style. In both MLA and APA styles, long quotations are double-spaced. You still need to integrate a block quotation into the text of your project by mentioning who wrote or said it.

WRITING SMART

Use quotations effectively

Quotations are a frequent problem area in research projects. Review every quotation to ensure that each is used effectively and correctly.

- **Check that each quotation is supporting your major points rather than making major points for you.** If the ideas rather than the original wording are what's important, paraphrase the quotation and cite the source.
- **Check that each quotation is introduced and attributed.** Each quotation should be introduced and the author or title named. Check for verbs that signal a quotation: Smith *claims*, Jones *argues*, Brown *states*.
- **Check that each quotation is properly formatted and punctuated.** Prose quotations longer than four lines (MLA) or forty words (APA) should be indented ten spaces in MLA style or five spaces in APA style. Shorter quotations should be enclosed within quotation marks.
- **Limit the use of long quotations.** If you have more than one block quotation on a page, look closely to see if one or more can be paraphrased or summarized. Use direct quotations only if the original wording is important.
- **Check that you cite the source for each quotation.** You are required to cite the sources of all direct quotations, paraphrases, and summaries.
- **Check the accuracy of each quotation.** It's easy to leave out words or mistype a quotation. Compare what is in your project with the original source. If you need to add words to make the quotation grammatical, make sure the added words are in brackets. Use ellipses to indicate omitted words.
- **Read your project aloud to a classmate or a friend.** Each quotation should flow smoothly when you read your project aloud. Put a checkmark beside rough spots as you read aloud so you can revise later.

- No quotation marks appear around the block quotation.
- Words quoted in the original retain the double quotation marks.
- The page number appears after the period at the end of the block quotation.

It is a good idea to include at least one or two sentences following the quotation to describe its significance to your thesis.

Double-check quotations

Whether they are long or short, you should double-check all quotations you use to be sure they are accurate and that all words belonging to the original are set off with quotation marks or placed in a block quotation. If you wish to leave out words from a quotation, indicate the omitted words with ellipses (. . .), but make sure you do not alter the meaning of the original quote (see Section 34e). If you need to add words of your own to a quotation to make the meaning clear, place your words in square brackets (see Section 34d).

 Use Summaries and Paraphrases Effectively

In many cases you will want to include the ideas and facts from a source, but the exact words from the source are not especially important. You still need to cite the source, but you will need to put the ideas and facts into your own words.

Summaries

A summary states the major ideas of an entire source or part of a source in a paragraph or perhaps even a sentence. The key is to put the summary in your own words. If you use words from the source, you have to put those words within quotation marks.

Gabriella Lopez wanted to establish that many college students are more aware of the benefits of healthy and sustainable food. She wanted to document that a trend is occurring by citing sources. She summarized an article in *USA Today* in one sentence (see p. 103).

> According to a 2006 article in *USA Today*, students are increasingly interested in schools with "green" practices, which offer local, sustainable, and organic options in their food service (Horovitz).

Paraphrases

Paraphrases represent the ideas in a source in your own words at about the same length as the original. You still need to include an in-text citation to the source. If you take words from the source, put them within quotation marks.

Gabriella wanted to give specifics about square-foot gardening in her research project. She paraphrased the discussion from Mel Bartholomew's *All New Square Foot Gardening*. The facts about square-foot gardening were important for her, but not the wording from the source (see pp. 107–108).

> I propose that we establish a campus garden following the very simple principles of organic "square-foot" gardening. Square-foot gardening is raised-bed gardening that takes place in 6- to 12-inch-deep frames that have been segmented into a grid (see Fig. 1). The size of each square in the grid depends on what plants are planted there; certain plants require larger and deeper grids (Bartholomew 15-16). The main benefit of square-foot gardening is that one can grow the same amount of produce in a 140-square-foot grid that is typically grown in the average 700-square-foot, single-row garden (42).

13 Understand and Avoid Plagiarism

QUICK*TAKE*

- Understand what is considered plagiarism (see below)
- Understand what sources need to be acknowledged (see p. 66)

13a What Is Plagiarism?

Plagiarism means claiming credit for someone else's intellectual work, no matter whether it's to make money or get a better grade. Intentional or not, plagiarism has dire consequences. Reputable authors have gotten into

trouble through carelessness by copying passages from published sources without acknowledging those sources. A number of famous people have had their reputations tarnished by accusations of plagiarism, and several prominent journalists have lost their jobs and careers for copying the work of other writers and passing it off as their own.

Deliberate plagiarism

If you buy a paper on the Web, copy someone else's paper word for word, or take an article off the Web and turn it in as yours, it's plain stealing, and people who take that risk should know that the punishment can be severe—usually failure for the course and sometimes expulsion. Deliberate plagiarism is easy for your instructors to spot because they recognize shifts in style, and it is easy for them to use search engines to find the sources of work stolen from the Web.

Patch plagiarism

The use of the Web has increased instances of plagiarism in college. Some students view the Internet as a big free buffet where they can grab anything, paste it into a file, and submit it as their own work. Other students intend to submit work that is their own, but they commit patch plagiarism because they aren't careful in taking notes to distinguish the words of others from their own words.

Original source

The economic advantage that has already begun to accrue to the walkable places can be attributed to three key factors. First, for certain segments of the population, chief among them young "creatives," urban living is simply more appealing; many wouldn't be caught dead anywhere else. Second, massive demographic shifts occurring right now mean that these pro-urban segments of the population are becoming dominant, creating a spike in demand that is expected to last for decades. Third, the choice to live the walkable life generates considerable savings for these households.

—Speck, Jeff. *Walkable City: How Downtown Can Save America One Step at a Time*. New York: Farrar, 2012. Print.

Patch plagiarism

The economic advantage gained by walkable places can be attributed to three key factors. First, for certain segments of the population, chief among them young "creatives," urban living is simply more appealing; many wouldn't be caught dead anywhere else. Second, young urban professionals are becoming dominant, creating a spike in demand that is expected to last for decades. Third, young professionals have figured out that they can save money by not owning a car. [Here phrases and an entire sentence highlighted in red are lifted from the original without quotation marks or acknowledgment of the source.]

 Which Sources Do You Need to Acknowledge?

What you are not required to acknowledge

Fortunately, common sense governs issues of academic plagiarism. The standards of documentation are not so strict that the source of every fact you cite must be acknowledged. You do not have to document the following.

- **Facts available from many sources.** For example, many reference sources report that the death toll of the sinking of the *Titanic* on April 15, 1912, was around 1,500.
- **Results of your own field research.** If you take a survey and report the results, you don't have to cite yourself. You do need to cite individual interviews.

What you are required to acknowledge

The following sources should be acknowledged with an in-text citation and an entry in the list of works cited (MLA style) or the list of references (APA style).

- **Quotations.** Short quotations should be enclosed within quotation marks, and long quotations should be indented as a block. See Section 12d for how to integrate quotations with signal phrases.
- **Summaries and paraphrases.** Summaries represent the author's argument in miniature as accurately as possible (see Section 12e). Paraphrases restate the author's argument in your own words.
- **Facts that are not common knowledge.** For facts that are not easily found in general reference works, cite the source.
- **Ideas that are not common knowledge.** The sources of theories, analyses, statements of opinion, and arguable claims should be cited.

- **Statistics, research findings, examples, graphs, charts, and illustrations.** As a reader you should be skeptical about statistics and research findings when the source is not mentioned. When a writer does not cite the sources of statistics and research findings, there is no way of knowing how reliable the sources are or whether the writer is making them up.

COMMON ERRORS

Plagiarism in college writing

If you find any of the following problems in your academic writing, you may be guilty of plagiarizing someone else's work. Because plagiarism is usually inadvertent, it is especially important that you understand what constitutes using sources responsibly. Avoid these pitfalls.

- **Missing attribution.** Make sure the author of a quotation has been identified. Include a lead-in or signal phrase that provides attribution to the source and identify the author in the citation.
- **Missing quotation marks.** You must put quotation marks around words quoted directly from a source.
- **Inadequate citation.** Give a page number to show where in the source the quotation appears or from where a paraphrase or summary is drawn.
- **Paraphrase relies too heavily on the source.** Be careful that the wording or sentence structure of a paraphrase does not follow the source too closely.
- **Distortion of meaning.** Don't allow your paraphrase or summary to distort the meaning of the source and don't take a quotation out of context, resulting in a change of meaning.
- **Missing works-cited entry.** The Works Cited page must include all the works cited in the project.
- **Inadequate citation of images.** A figure or photo must appear with a caption and a citation to indicate the source of the image. If material includes a summary of data from a visual source, an attribution or citation must be given for the graphic being summarized.

14 MLA Documentation

QUICK*TAKE*

- Use in-text citations in MLA style (see pp. 74–77)
- Create citations in the list of works cited (see pp. 78–102)
- Format a paper in MLA style (see pp. 102–113)

MLA Documentation Map

1 Collect the right Information

For every source you need to have

- the name of the author or authors,
- the full title, and
- complete publication information.

For instructions, go to the illustrated examples in Section 14d of the four major source types:

- **PRINTED ARTICLE**
- **PRINTED BOOK**
- **DATABASE PUBLICATION**
- **WEB PUBLICATION**

For other kinds of sources, such as visual and multimedia sources, see the Index of Works-Cited Entries on pp. 86–87.

2 Cite sources in two places

Remember, this is a two-part process.

To create citations

(a) in **the body of your paper**, go to 14a and 14c.

(b) in a **List of Works Cited at the end of your paper**, go to 14b.

Research writing requires you to document the sources of all of your information that is not common knowledge. The style developed by the Modern Language Association (MLA) requires you to document each source in two places: an in-text citation in the body of your project and a list of works cited at the end. If your readers want to find the source of a fact or quotation in your project, they can use your in-text citation to find the full information about a source in your works-cited list.

If you have questions that the examples in this chapter do not address, consult the *MLA Handbook for Writers of Research Papers*, seventh edition (2009), and the *MLA Style Manual and Guide to Scholarly Publishing*, third edition (2008).

3 | Find the right model citations

You'll find **illustrated examples of sources** in 14d.

Once you match your source to one of those examples, you can move on to more specific examples:

- **PRINTED ARTICLE,** go to 14e.
- **PRINTED BOOK** or parts of a book, go to 14f.
- **ONLINE:** was the source
  (a) in a **library database?** Go to 14g.
  (b) from **another Web source?** Go to 14h.

A complete list of examples is found in the Index of Works-Cited Entries on pp. 86–87.

4 | Format your paper

You'll find a **sample research paper in MLA style** and instructions on formatting the body of your paper and your works-cited list in 14k.

A note about footnotes:
MLA style does not use footnotes for documentation. Use in-text citations instead (see 14a and 14c). The only use of footnotes in MLA style is for providing additional information.

14a Citing Sources in an MLA-style Project

Gabriella Lopez chose to make a proposal argument for a campus garden as her research project. You can see the complete paper in Section 14k at the end of this chapter.

How to quote and cite a source in the text of an MLA-style paper

Gabriella searched for an article on the *PsycARTICLES* database using the search terms "food," "college students," and "health attitudes." She found the article below, and she printed a copy.

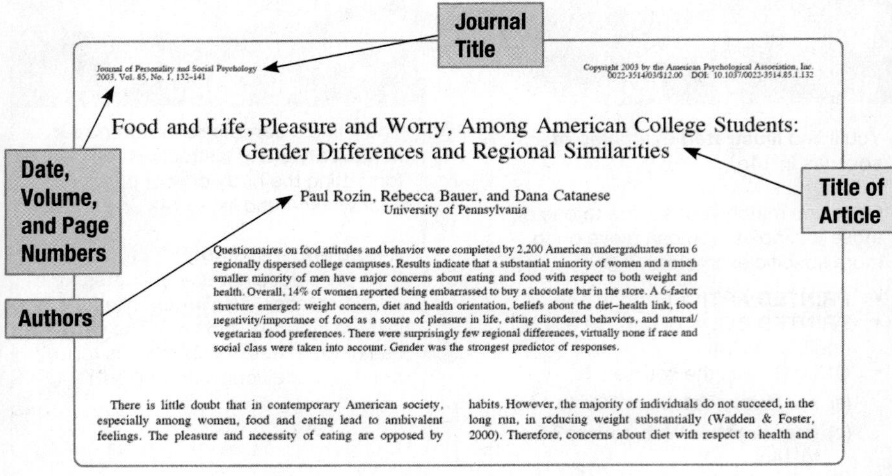
Journal of Personality and Social Psychology
2003, Vol. 85, No. 1, 132–141

Copyright 2003 by the American Psychological Association, Inc.
0022-3514/03/$12.00 DOI: 10.1037/0022-3514.85.1.132

Food and Life, Pleasure and Worry, Among American College Students: Gender Differences and Regional Similarities

Paul Rozin, Rebecca Bauer, and Dana Catanese
University of Pennsylvania

Questionnaires on food attitudes and behavior were completed by 2,200 American undergraduates from 6 regionally dispersed college campuses. Results indicate that a substantial minority of women and a much smaller minority of men have major concerns about eating and food with respect to both weight and health. Overall, 14% of women reported being embarrassed to buy a chocolate bar in the store. A 6-factor structure emerged: weight concern, diet and health orientation, beliefs about the diet–health link, food negativity/importance of food as a source of pleasure in life, eating disordered behaviors, and natural/vegetarian food preferences. There were surprisingly few regional differences, virtually none if race and social class were taken into account. Gender was the strongest predictor of responses.

There is little doubt that in contemporary American society, especially among women, food and eating lead to ambivalent feelings. The pleasure and necessity of eating are opposed by habits. However, the majority of individuals do not succeed, in the long run, in reducing weight substantially (Wadden & Foster, 2000). Therefore, concerns about diet with respect to health and

To support her argument that many students are concerned about what they eat, she decided to include a short quotation that points to the benefits of a healthy relationship with food.

Gabriella can either (a) mention Paul Rozin, Rebecca Bauer, and Dana Catanese in the text of her paper with a signal phrase or (b) place the authors' names inside parentheses following the quotation. Either with or without the signal phrase, in most cases she must include inside parentheses the page number where she found the quotation.

Author's name in signal phrase

> Paul Rozin, Rebecca Bauer, and Dana Catanese found in a survey of 2,200 American college students that a significant number of women and a smaller group of men have "major concerns about eating and food with respect to both weight and health" (132).

OR

Author's name in parenthetical citation

> According to a survey of 2,200 American college students, a significant number of women and a smaller group of men have "major concerns about eating and food with respect to both weight and health" (Rozin, Bauer, and Catanese 132).

If Gabriella includes a quotation that is four lines or longer, she must double-space and indent the quotation in her paper 1 inch (see example on pp. 105–106).

Include in-text citations for summaries and paraphrases

In another paragraph, Gabriella summarized Bartholomew's recommendations and gave the page numbers from that source.

> The size of each square in the grid depends on what plants are planted there; certain plants require larger and deeper grids (Bartholomew 15-16). The main benefit of square-foot gardening is that one can grow the same amount of produce in a 140-square-foot grid that is typically grown in the average 700-square-foot, single-row garden (42).

14b Creating the List of Works Cited

Gabriella is ready to create an entry for the list of Works Cited at the end of her paper.

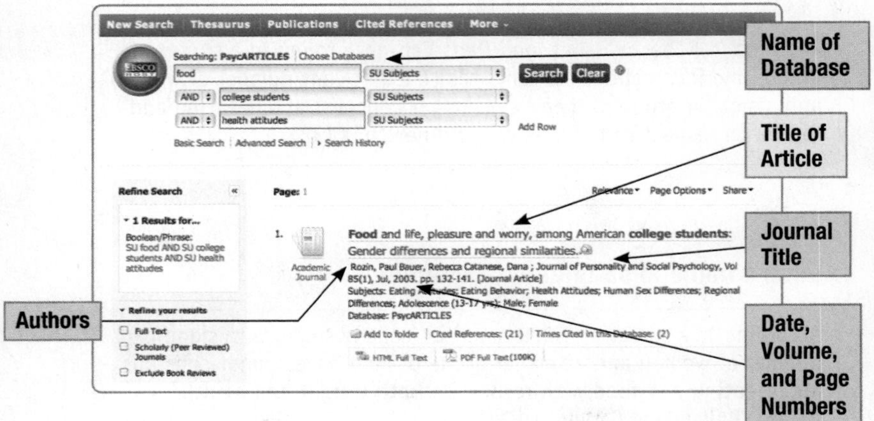

Gabriella asked herself a series of questions to create an entry for this source in her list of Works Cited.

1. ***What information do I need to pull from this screenshot?***

   For a source like this article from an online database, she needs to know five things: (1) what type of source it is; (2) the author; (3) the title; (4) the publication information; and (5) information about the online database.

2. ***I know this is from my library's online database, but that could be one of several different types of sources. What kind of source is this?***

   Gabriella selected the database *PsycARTICLES* for her search; thus, she knew that her source type would be an article.

3. ***Now how do I find the author's name?***

   Look for a bold heading that says something like "AUTHOR" or "BYLINE." If more than one author is listed, take note of all names listed.

4. ***What is the title of my source?***

   If the title is not immediately evident, look for a heading that says "TITLE" or "HEADLINE."

5. ***Where do I find the publication information?***

   The name and date of the periodical are usually listed at the top of the page but are sometimes found at the bottom.

6. ***Where do I find the name of the database?***

   For databases distributed by EBSCO, you have to look for the name of the database. EBSCO is the vendor who sells access to many databases such as *PsycARTICLES.*

Gabriella listed the information.

AUTHORS	*Rozin, Paul, Rebecca Bauer, and Dana Catanese*
TITLE OF ARTICLE	*"Food and Life, Pleasure and Worry, among American College Students: Gender Differences and Regional Similarities"*
PUBLICATION INFORMATION	
Name of periodical	*Journal of Personality and Social Psychology*
Volume, date of publication, and page number	*85.1 (2003): 132-41*
DATABASE INFORMATION	
Name of database	*PsycARTICLES*
Date the site was accessed	*20 Apr. 2013*

Then she used the instructions on page 83 to format her citation.

Lopez 10

Works Cited

Rozin, Paul, Rebecca Bauer, and Dana Catanese. "Food and Life, Pleasure and Worry, among American College Students: Gender Differences and Regional Similarities." *Journal of Personality and Social Psychology* 85.1 (2003): 132–41. *PsycARTICLES.* Web. 20 Apr. 2013.

14c In-text Citations in MLA Style

Index of in-text citations

1. Author named in a signal phrase

Put the author's name in a signal phrase in your sentence.

> Sociologist Daniel Bell called this emerging U.S. economy the "postindustrial society" (3).

2. Author not named in your text

> In 2012, the Gallup poll reported that 56% of adults in the United States think secondhand smoke is "very harmful," compared to only 36% in 1994 (Saad 4).

3. Work by one author

The author's last name comes first, followed by the page number. There is no comma.

(Bell 3)

4. Work by two or three authors

The authors' last names follow the order of the title page. If there are two authors, join the names with *and.* If there are three, use a comma between the first two names and a comma with *and* before the last name.

(Francisco, Vaughn, and Lynn 7)

5. Work by four or more authors

You may use the phrase *et al.* (meaning "and others") for all names but the first, or you may write out all the names. Make sure you use the same method for both the in-text citations and the works-cited list.

(Abrams et al. 1653)

6. Author unknown

Use a shortened version of the title that includes at least the first important word. Your reader will use the shortened title to find the full title in the works-cited list.

A review in the *New Yorker* of Ryan Adams's new album focuses on the artist's age ("Pure" 25).

Notice that "Pure" is in quotation marks because it is the shortened title of an article. If it were a book, the short title would be in italics.

7. Quotations longer than four lines

NOTE: When using indented ("block") quotations that are longer than four lines, the period appears *before* the parentheses enclosing the page number.

In her article "Art for Everybody," Susan Orlean attempts to explain the popularity of painter Thomas Kinkade:

> People like to own things they think are valuable. . . . The high price of limited editions is part of their appeal: it implies that they are choice and exclusive, and that only a certain class of people will be able to afford them. (128)

This same statement could also explain the popularity of phenomena like PBS's *Antiques Road Show*.

8. Two or more works by the same author

Use the author's last name and then a shortened version of the title of each source.

The majority of books written about coauthorship focus on partners of the same sex (Laird, *Women* 351).

Note that *Women* is italicized because it is the title of a book.

9. Different authors with the same last name

Include the initial of the first name in the parenthetical reference.

Web surfing requires more mental involvement than channel surfing (S. Johnson 107).

10. Two or more sources within the same citation

If two sources support a single point, separate them with a semicolon.

(McKibbin 39; Gore 92)

11. Work quoted in another source

When you do not have access to the original source of the material you wish to use and only an indirect source is available, put the abbreviation *qtd. in* ("quoted in") before the information about the indirect source.

> National governments have become increasingly what Ulrich Beck, in a 1999 interview, calls "zombie institutions"—institutions that are "dead and still alive" (qtd. in Bauman 6).

12. One-page source

A page reference is unnecessary when you are citing a one-page work.

> Economists agree that automating routine work is the broad goal of globalization (Lohr).

13. Online sources including Web pages, blogs, podcasts, tweets, social media, wikis, videos, and other multimedia sources

MLA prefers that you mention the author in your text instead of putting the author's name in parentheses.

> Andrew Keen ironically used his own blog to claim that "blogs are boring to write (yawn), boring to read (yawn) and boring to discuss (yawn)."

14. Classic works

To supply a reference to classic works, you sometimes need more than a page number from a specific edition. Readers should be able to locate a quotation in any edition of the book. Give the page number from the edition that you are using, then a semicolon and other identifying information.

> "Marriage is a house" is one of the most memorable lines in *Don Quixote* (546; pt. 2, bk. 3, ch. 19).

14d Illustrated Samples and Index of Works-Cited Entries in MLA Style

Printed Article

Scholarly journals usually list the publication information at the top or bottom of the first page. Popular magazines often do not list volume and issue numbers. You can find the date of publication on the cover.

Ecological Applications, 17(6), 2007, pp. 1742–1751
© 2007 by the Ecological Society of America

A CROSS-REGIONAL ASSESSMENT OF THE FACTORS AFFECTING ECOLITERACY: IMPLICATIONS FOR POLICY AND PRACTICE

Sarah Pilgrim, David Smith, and Jules Pretty[1]

Centre for Environment and Society, Department of Biological Sciences, University of Essex, Wivenhoe Park, Colchester CO4 3SQ United Kingdom

Abstract. The value of accumulated ecological knowledge, termed ecoliteracy, is vital to both human and ecosystem health. Maintenance of this knowledge is essential for continued support of local conservation efforts and the capacity of communities to self- or co-manage their local resources sustainably. Most previous studies have been qualitative and small scale, documenting ecoliteracy in geographically isolated locations. In this study, we take a different approach, focusing on (1) the primary factors affecting individual levels of ecoliteracy, (2) whether these factors shift with economic development, and (3) if different knowledge protection strategies are required for the future. We compared non-resource-dependent communities in the United Kingdom with resource-dependent communities in India and Indonesia (n = 1250 interviews). We found that UK residents with the highest levels of ecoliteracy visited the countryside frequently, lived and grew up in rural areas, and acquired their knowledge from informal word-of-mouth sources, such as parents and friends, rather than television and schooling. The ecoliteracy of resource-dependent community members, however, varied with wealth status and gender. The least wealthy families depended most on local resources for their livelihoods and had the highest levels of ecoliteracy. Gender roles affected both the level and content of an individual's ecoliteracy. The importance of reciprocal oral transfer of this knowledge in addition to direct experience to the maintenance of ecoliteracy was apparent at all sites. Lessons learned may contribute to new local resource management strategies for combined ecoliteracy conservation. Without novel policies, local community management capacity is likely to be depleted in the future.

Key words: ecoliteracy; India; Indonesia; knowledge; natural resource; oral traditions; resource management; sustainable management; United Kingdom.

Citation in the List of Works Cited

Pilgrim, Sarah, David Smith, and Jules Pretty. "A Cross-Regional Assessment of the Factors Affecting Ecoliteracy: Implications for Policy and Practice." *Ecological Applications* 17.6 (2007): 1742-51. Print.

Elements of the citation

Author's Name

The author's last name comes first, followed by a comma and the first name.

For two or more works by the same author, see page 92.

Title of Article

Use the exact title and put it inside quotation marks. If a book title is part of the article's title, italicize the book title.

Publication Information

Name of journal or newspaper Italicize the title of the journal or newspaper.

Abbreviate the title if it commonly appears that way.

Volume, issue, and page numbers For scholarly journals give the volume number and issue number. Place a period between the volume and issue numbers: "55.3" indicates volume 55, issue 3.

Some scholarly journals use issue numbers only.

Give the page numbers for the entire article, not just the part you used.

Medium of publication Print.

Find the right example for your model (you may need to refer to more than one model)

What type of article do you have?

A scholarly journal article?

Go to page 89, #22–23.

A newspaper article, review, editorial, or letter to the editor?

- For a newspaper article, go to pages 90–91, #27–31.
- For a review, go to page 91, #32.
- For an editorial, go to page 91, #34.
- For a letter to the editor, go to page 91, #33.

A government document?

Go to page 91, #35–36.

How many authors are listed?

- One, two, or more authors: go to page 88, #15–17.
- Unknown author: go to page 88, #18.

What kind of pagination is used?

- For a scholarly journal, go to page 89, #22.
- For a journal that starts every issue with page 1, go to page 89, #23.

Printed Book

Find the copyright date on the copyright page, which is on the back of the title page. Use the copyright date for the date of publication, not the date of printing.

Citation in the List of Works Cited

Pollan, Michael. *In Defense of Food: An Eater's Manifesto*. New York: Penguin, 2008. Print.

Elements of the citation

Author's or Editor's Name

The author's last name comes first, followed by a comma and the first name.

For edited books, put the abbreviation *ed.* after the name, preceded by a comma:
Kavanagh, Peter, ed.

Book Title

Use the exact title, as it appears on the title page (not the cover).

Italicize the title.

Publication Information

Place of publication
If more than one city is given, use the first.

For cities outside the United States, add an abbreviation of the country or province if the city is not well known.

Publisher
Omit words such as *Publisher* and *Inc*.

For university presses, use *UP*: New York UP

Shorten the name. For example, shorten *W. W. Norton & Co*. to *Norton*.

Date of publication
Give the year as it appears on the copyright page.

Otherwise, put *n.d.* ("no date"): Cambridge: Harvard UP, n.d.

Medium of publication
Print.

Find the right example for your model (you may need to refer to more than one model)

How many authors are listed?

- One, two, or more authors: go to page 92, #38–41.
- Unknown author: go to page 93, #42.
- Group or organization as the author: go to page 93, #43.

Do you have only a part of a book?

- For an introduction, foreword, preface, or afterword, go to page 93, #44.
- For a chapter in an anthology or edited collection, go to page 93, #45.
- For more than one selection in an anthology or edited collection, go to page 93, #46.

Do you have two or more books by the same author?

- Go to page 92, #39.

Library Database Publication

You will find library databases linked from your library's Web site.

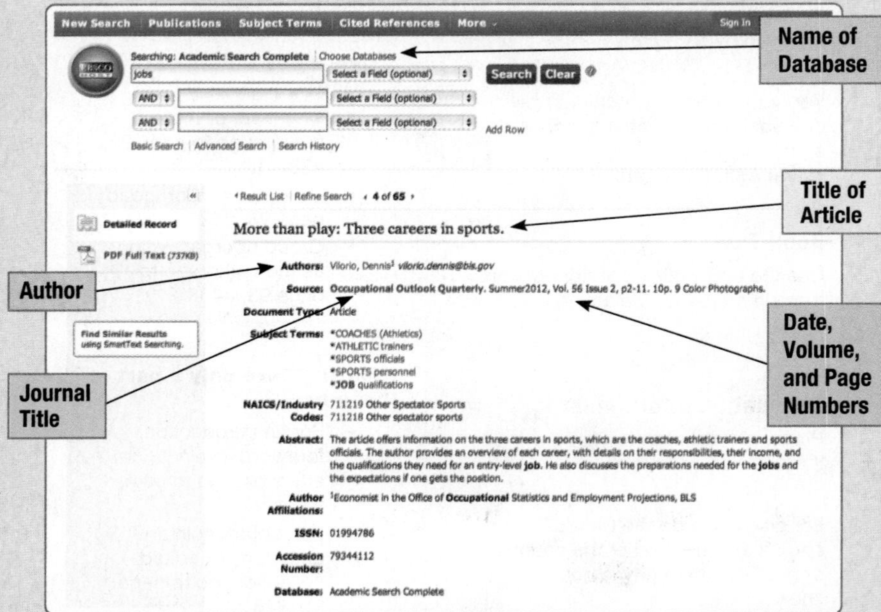

Citation in the List of Works Cited

Vilorio, Dennis. "More than Play: Three Careers in Sports." *Occupational Outlook Quarterly* 56.2 (2012): 2-11. *Academic Search Complete*. Web. 8 Apr. 2014.

Take Note

Don't confuse the name of the vendor—the company that sells access to the database—with the name of the database. For example, EBSCO or EBSCO Host is not the name of a database but the name of the vendor that sells access to databases such as *Academic Search Complete.*

Elements of the citation

Start with the citation with the exact format for a print citation. Replace the word *Print* at the end with the name of the database, the medium (*Web*), and the date you accessed the source.

Author's Name

The author's last name comes first, followed by a comma and the first name.

Title of Source

Use the exact title and put it inside quotation marks.

Publication Information for an Article

Name of journal or newspaper
Italicize the title of the journal or newspaper. Abbreviate the title if it commonly appears that way.

Volume, issue, date, and page numbers
List the same information you would for a print item. If there are no page numbers, put *n. pag.* where the page numbers would ordinarily go.

Database Information

Name of the database
Italicize the name of the database, followed by a period.

Medium of publication
For all database sources, the medium of publication is *Web*.

Date of access
List the date you accessed the source (day, month, year).

Find the right example for your model (you may need to refer to more than one model)

Most databases allow you to search by document type, such as scholarly journal, newspaper article, financial report, legal case, or abstract. Use these categories to identify the type of publication.

What kind of publication do you have?

- For an article in a scholarly journal, go to page 95, #55
- For a magazine article, go to page 95, #56
- For a newspaper article, go to page 95, #58
- For a legal case, go to page 95, #59

Do you have a publication with an unknown author?

Go to page 95, #57.

Web Publication

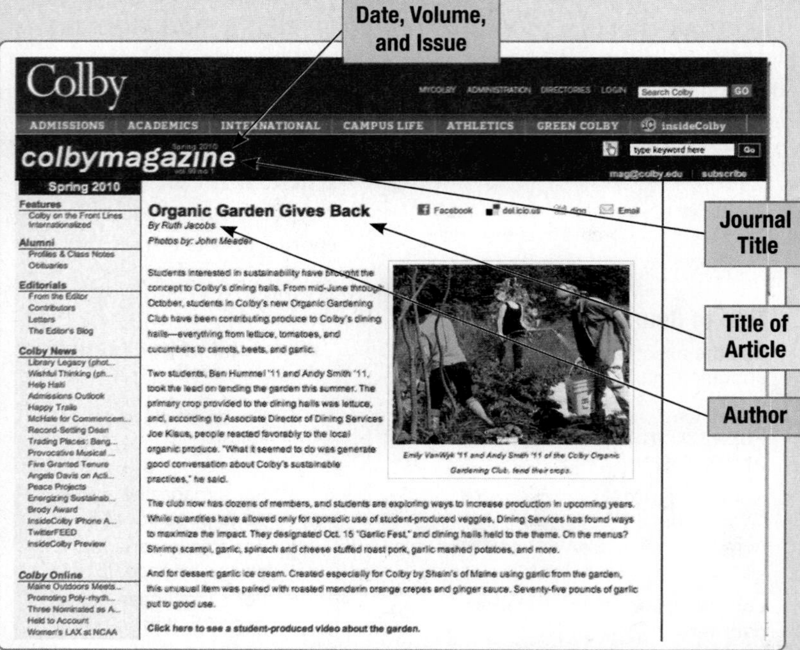

Organic Garden Gives Back

By Ruth Jacobs

Photos by: John Meader

Students interested in sustainability have brought the concept to Colby's dining halls. From mid-June through October, students in Colby's new Organic Gardening Club have been contributing produce to Colby's dining halls—everything from lettuce, tomatoes, and cucumbers to carrots, beets, and garlic.

Two students, Ben Hummel '11 and Andy Smith '11, took the lead on tending the garden this summer. The primary crop provided to the dining halls was lettuce, and, according to Associate Director of Dining Services Joe Klaus, people reacted favorably to the local organic produce. "What it seemed to do was generate good conversation about Colby's sustainable practices," he said.

Emily VanWyk '11 and Andy Smith '11 of the Colby Organic Gardening Club, tend their crops.

The club now has dozens of members, and students are exploring ways to increase production in upcoming years. While quantities have allowed only for sporadic use of student-produced veggies, Dining Services has found ways to maximize the impact. They designated Oct. 15 "Garlic Fest," and dining halls held to the theme. On the menus? Shrimp scampi, garlic, spinach and cheese stuffed roast pork, garlic mashed potatoes, and more.

And for dessert: garlic ice cream. Created especially for Colby by Shain's of Maine using garlic from the garden, this unusual item was paired with roasted mandarin orange crepes and ginger sauce. Seventy-five pounds of garlic put to good use.

Click here to see a student-produced video about the garden.

Citation in the List of Works Cited

Jacobs, Ruth. "Organic Garden Gives Back." *Colby Magazine* 99.1 (2010): n. pag. Web. 2 Apr. 2014.

When Do You List a URL?

MLA style no longer requires including URLs of Web sources. URLs are of limited value because they change frequently and they can be specific to an individual search. Include the URL as supplementary information only when your readers probably cannot locate the source without the URL.

Elements of the citation

Author's Name

Authorship is sometimes hard to discern for online sources. If you know the author or creator, follow the rules for books and journals.

If the only authority you find is a group or organization, list its name after the date of publication or last revision.

Title of Source

Place the title of the work inside quotation marks if it is part of a larger Web site.

Untitled works may be identified by a label (e.g., *Home page, Introduction*). List the label in the title slot without quotation marks or italics.

Italicize the name of the overall site if it is different from the work. The name of the overall Web site will usually be found on its index or home page.

Some Web sites are updated, so list the version if you find it (e.g., *Vers. 1.2*).

Publication Information for Web Sources

List the publisher's or sponsor's name, followed by a comma. If it isn't available, use *N.p.*

List the date of publication by day, month, and year if available. If you cannot find a date, use *n.d.*

Give the medium of publication (*Web*).

List the date you accessed the site by day, month, and year.

Find the right example for your model (you may need to refer to more than one model)

Do you have a Web page or an entire Web site?

- For an entire Web site, go to page 96, #61
- For a page on a Web site, go to page 96, #60

What kind of publication do you have, and who is the author?

- For a known author, go to page 96, #62
- For a group or organization as the author, go to page 96, #63
- For a publication with print publication data, go to page 96, #64
- For an article in a scholarly journal, newspaper, or magazine, go to page 97, #65–67

Do you have a source that is posted by an individual?

- For a posting on social media, go to page 98, #71
- For a posting on *Twitter*, go to page 98, #72
- For e-mail or text messaging, go to page 99, #74
- For a post to a discussion list, go to page 99, #75
- For a blog, go to page 99, #77

Index of Works Cited Entries

14e Journals, Magazines, Newspapers, and Other Print Sources 88

14f Books 92

14g Library Database Sources 95

14h Web Sources and Other Online Sources 96

Web sites

Publications on the Web

Periodicals on the Web

Digital Books, Archives, and Government Publications

Unedited Online Sources

14i Visual Sources 99

Visual Sources on the Web

14j Multimedia Sources 101

14e Journals, Magazines, Newspapers, and Other Print Sources

JOURNAL AND MAGAZINE ARTICLES

15. Article by one author

Ekotto, Frieda. "Against Representation: Countless Hours for a Professor." *PMLA* 127.4 (2012): 968-72. Print.

16. Article by two or three authors

The second and subsequent authors' names are printed first name first.

Condon, William, and Carol Rutz. "A Taxonomy of Writing across the Curriculum Programs: Evolving to Serve Broader Agendas." *CCC* 64.2 (2012): 357-82. Print.

Notice that a comma separates the authors' names.

17. Article by four or more authors

You may use the phrase *et al.* (meaning "and others") for all authors but the first, or you may write out all the names.

Breece, Katherine E., et al. "Patterns of mtDNA Diversity in Northwestern North America." *Human Biology* 76.5 (2004): 33-54. Print.

18. Article by an unknown author

Begin the entry with the title.

"Light Box." *Time* 28 Jan. 2013: 6-7. Print.

19. Article with a title within a title

If the title of the article contains the title of another short work, include it in single quotation marks. Italicize a title or a word that would normally be italicized.

Happel, Alison, and Jennifer Esposito. "Vampires, Vixens, and Feminists: An Analysis of *Twilight*." *Educational Studies* 46.5 (2010): 524-31. Print.

MONTHLY, WEEKLY, AND BIWEEKLY MAGAZINES

20. Monthly or seasonal magazines or journals

Use the month (or season) and year in place of the volume. Abbreviate the names of all months except May, June, and July.

> Huang, Yasheng. "China's Other Path." *Wilson Quarterly* Spring 2010: 58-64. Print.

21. Weekly or biweekly magazines

For weekly or biweekly magazines, give both the day and month of publication, as listed on the issue.

> Thurman, Judith. "Ask Betty." *New Yorker* 11 Nov. 2012: 40-43. Print.

DIFFERENT TYPES OF PAGINATION

22. Article in a scholarly journal

List the volume and issue numbers after the name of the journal.

> Bernard-Donals, Michael. "Synecdochic Memory at the United States Holocaust Memorial Museum." *College English* 74.5 (2012): 417-36. Print.

23. Article in a scholarly journal that uses only issue numbers

If a journal begins each issue on page 1, list the issue number after the name of the journal.

> McCall, Sophie. "Double Vision Reading." *Canadian Literature* 194 (2007): 95-97. Print.

REVIEWS, EDITORIALS, LETTERS TO THE EDITOR

24. Review

Provide the title, if given, and name the work reviewed. If there is no title, just name the work reviewed. For film reviews, name the director.

> Mendelsohn, Daniel. "The Two Oscar Wildes." Rev. of *The Importance of Being Earnest*, dir. Oliver Parker. *New York Review of Books* 10 Oct. 2002: 23-24. Print.

25. Letter to the editor

Add the word *Letter* after the name of the author.

Patai, Daphne. Letter. *Harper's* Dec. 2001: 4. Print.

26. Editorial

If the editorial is unsigned, put the title first. Add the word *Editorial* after the title.

"Stop Stonewalling on Reform." Editorial. *Business Week* 17 June 2002: 108. Print.

NEWSPAPER ARTICLES

27. Article by one author

Rojas, Rick. "For Young Sikhs, a Tie That Binds Them to Their Faith." *Washington Post* 20 June 2010, final ed.: C03. Print.

28. Article by two or three authors

The second and subsequent authors' names are printed in regular order, first name first:

Chazen, Guy, and Dana Cimilluca. "BP Amasses Cash for Oil-Spill Costs." *Wall Street Journal* 26 June 2010: A1. Print.

Notice that a comma separates the authors' names.

29. Article by four or more authors

You may use the phrase *et al.* (meaning "and others") for all authors but the first, or you may write out all the names. Use the same method in the in-text citation as you do in the works-cited list.

Watson, Anne, et al. "Childhood Obesity on the Rise." *Daily Missoulian* 7 July 2003: B1. Print.

30. Article by an unknown author

Begin the entry with the title.

"Missile Launcher Turns Up at Buyback." *Austin American-Statesman* 21 Jan. 2013: A7. Print.

31. Article that continues to a nonconsecutive page

Add a plus sign after the number of the first page.

Kaplow, Larry, and Tasgola Karla Bruner. "U.S.: Don't Let Taliban Forces Flee." *Austin American-Statesman* 20 Nov. 2001, final ed.: A11+. Print.

NEWSPAPER REVIEWS, EDITORIALS, LETTERS TO THE EDITOR

32. Review

List the reviewer's name and the title of the review. Then write *Rev. of*, followed by the title of the work, the word *by*, and the author's name.

Garner, Dwight. "Violence Expert Visits Her Dark Past?" Rev. of *Denial: A Memoir of Terror*, by Jessica Stern. *New York Times* 25 June 2010, natl. ed.: 28. Print.

33. Letter to the editor

Leach, Richard E. Letter. *Boston Globe* 2 Apr. 2007, first ed.: A10. Print.

34. Editorial

If the editorial is unsigned, put the title first.

"High Court Ruling Doesn't Mean Vouchers Will Work." Editorial. *Atlanta Journal and Constitution* 28 June 2002, home ed.: A19. Print.

GOVERNMENT DOCUMENTS

35. Government document

United States. General Services Administration. *Consumer Action Handbook.* Washington: GPO, 2008. Print.

36. *Congressional Record*

Cong. Rec. 8 Feb. 2000: 1222-46. Print.

DISSERTATIONS

37. Published dissertation or thesis

Mason, Jennifer. *Civilized Creatures: Animality, Cultural Power, and American Literature, 1850-1901*. Diss. U of Texas at Austin, 2000. Ann Arbor: UMI, 2000. Print.

14f Books

ONE AUTHOR

38. Book by one author

Mayer-Schönberger, Viktor. *Delete: The Virtue of Forgetting in the Digital Age*. Princeton: Princeton UP, 2009. Print.

39. Two or more books by the same author

In the entry for the first book, include the author's name. In the second entry, substitute three hyphens and a period for the author's name. List the titles of books by the same author in alphabetical order.

Krakauer, Jon. *Into the Wild*. New York: Villard, 1996. Print.

---. *Where Men Win Glory: The Odyssey of Pat Tillman*. New York: Doubleday, 2009. Print.

MULTIPLE AUTHORS

40. Book by two or three authors

The second and subsequent authors' names appear first name first.

Burger, Edward B., and Michael Starbird. *Coincidences, Chaos, and All That Math Jazz*. New York: Norton, 2006. Print.

41. Book by four or more authors

You may use the phrase *et al.* (meaning "and others") for all authors but the first, or you may write out all the names. Use the same method in the in-text citation as you do in the works-cited list.

North, Stephen M., et al. *Refiguring the Ph.D. in English Studies*. Urbana: NCTE, 2000. Print.

ANONYMOUS AND GROUP AUTHORS

42. Book by an unknown author

Begin the entry with the title.

Encyclopedia of Americana. New York: Somerset, 2001. Print.

43. Book by a group or organization

Treat the group as the author of the work.

United Nations. *The Charter of the United Nations: A Commentary*. New York: Oxford UP, 2000. Print.

PARTS OF BOOKS

44. Introduction, foreword, preface, or afterword

Benstock, Sheri. Introduction. *The House of Mirth*. By Edith Wharton. Boston: Bedford-St. Martin's, 2002. 3-24. Print.

45. Chapter in an anthology or edited collection

Sedaris, David. "Full House." *The Best American Nonrequired Reading 2004*. Ed. Dave Eggers. Boston: Houghton, 2004. 350-58. Print.

46. More than one selection from an anthology or edited collection

Multiple selections from a single anthology can be handled by creating a complete entry for the anthology and shortened cross-references for individual works in that anthology.

Adichie, Chimamanda Ngozi. "Half of a Yellow Sun." Eggers 1-17.

Eggers, Dave, ed. *The Best American Nonrequired Reading 2004*. Boston: Houghton, 2004. Print.

Sedaris, David. "Full House." Eggers 350-58.

47. Article in a reference work

"Utilitarianism." *The Columbia Encyclopedia*. 6th ed. 2001. Print.

THE BIBLE AND OTHER SACRED TEXTS

48. Sacred texts

The New Oxford Annotated Bible. Ed. Bruce M. Metzger and Roland E. Murphy. New York: Oxford UP, 1991. Print.

Use a period to separate the chapter and verse in the in-text note: (John 3.16)

EDITIONS, TRANSLATIONS, AND ILLUSTRATED BOOKS

49. Book with an editor—focus on the editor

Lewis, Gifford, ed. *The Big House of Inver*. By Edith Somerville and Martin Ross. Dublin: Farmar, 2000. Print.

50. Book with an editor—focus on the author

Somerville, Edith, and Martin Ross. *The Big House of Inver*. Ed. Gifford Lewis. Dublin: Farmar, 2000. Print.

51. Book with a translator

Mallarmé, Stéphane. *Divagations*. 1897. Trans. Barbara Johnson. Cambridge: Harvard UP, 2007. Print.

52. Second or subsequent edition of a book

Hawthorn, Jeremy, ed. *A Concise Glossary of Contemporary Literary Theory*. 3rd ed. London: Arnold, 2001. Print.

53. Illustrated book or graphic narrative

After the title of the book, give the illustrator's name, preceded by the abbreviation *Illus.* If the emphasis is on the illustrator's work, place the illustrator's name first, followed by the abbreviation *illus.*, and list the author after the title, preceded by the word *By*.

Strunk, William, Jr., and E. B. White. *The Elements of Style Illustrated*. Illus. Maira Kalman. New York: Penguin, 2005. Print.

MULTIVOLUME WORKS

54. One volume of a multivolume work

Samuel, Raphael. *Theatres of Memory*. Vol. 1. London: Verso, 1999. Print.

14g Library Database Sources

Give the print citation, followed by the name of the database in italics, the medium (*Web*), and the date you accessed the database. You do not need to list the URL of common library databases.

55. Scholarly journal article from a library database

Klesges, Robert C., Mary L. Shelton, and Lisa M. Klesges. "Effects of Television on Metabolic Rate: Potential Implications for Childhood Obesity." *Pediatrics* 91 (1993): 281-86. *Academic Search Complete*. Web. 14 Nov. 2013.

56. Magazine article from a library database

"The Trouble with Immortality: If We Could Live Forever, Would We Really Want To?" *Newsweek* 5 July 2010, US ed.: 78. *Academic Search Complete*. Web. 9 Dec. 2013.

57. Article with unknown author from a library database

"Dicing with Data: Facebook, Google and Privacy." *Economist* 22 May 2010, US ed.: 16. *LexisNexis Academic*. Web. 15 Sept. 2013.

58. Newspaper article from a library database

Franciane, Valerie. "Quarter Is Ready to Rock." *Times-Picayune* [New Orleans] 3 Apr. 2007: 1. *LexisNexis Academic*. Web. 23 Jan. 2014.

59. Legal case from a library database

Bilski v. Kappos. 561 US 08-964. Supreme Court of the US. 28 June 2010. *LexisNexis Academic*. Web. 28 June 2014.

14h Web Sources and Other Online Sources

WEB SITES

60. Page on a Web site

The basic format for citing a Web page includes the author or editor, the title of the page, the title of the site (in italics), the sponsor or publisher of the site, the date of publication, the medium (*Web*), and the date you accessed the site.

Boerner, Steve. "Leopold Mozart." *The Mozart Project: Biography*. Mozart Project, 21 Mar. 1998. Web. 30 Oct. 2014.

61. Entire Web site

Boerner, Steve. *The Mozart Project*. Mozart Project, 20 July 2007. Web. 30 Oct. 2014.

PUBLICATIONS ON THE WEB

62. Publication by a known author

Samadzadeh, Nozlee. "Farm Update: The Third Annual Jack Hitt Annual Last Day of Classes Pig Roast." *Yale Sustainable Food Project Student Blog*. Yale Sustainable Food Project, 3 May 2010. Web. 10 May 2014.

63. Publication by a group or organization

If a work has no author's or editor's name listed, begin the entry with the title.

"State of the Birds." *Audubon*. Natl. Audubon Society, 2012. Web. 19 Aug. 2013.

64. Publication on the Web with print publication data

Include the print publication information. Then give the name of the Web site or database in italics, the medium of publication (*Web*), and the date of access (day, month, and year).

Kirsch, Irwin S., et al. *Adult Literacy in America*. Darby: Diane, 1993. *Google Scholar*. Web. 30 Oct. 2010.

PERIODICALS ON THE WEB

65. Article in a scholarly journal on the Web

Some scholarly journals are published on the Web only. List articles by author, title, name of journal in italics, volume and issue number, and year of publication. If the journal does not have page numbers, use *n. pag.* in place of page numbers. Then list the medium of publication (*Web*) and the date of access (day, month, and year).

Fleckenstein, Kristie. "Who's Writing? Aristotelian Ethos and the Author Position in Digital Poetics." *Kairos* 11.3 (2007): n. pag. Web. 6 Apr. 2014.

66. Article in a newspaper on the Web

List the name of the newspaper in italics, followed by a period and the publisher's name. Follow the publisher's name with a comma. The first date is the date of publication; the second is the date of access.

Brown, Patricia Leigh. "Australia in Sonoma." *New York Times*. New York Times, 5 July 2008. Web. 3 Aug. 2013.

67. Article in a popular magazine on the Web

Brown, Patricia Leigh. "The Wild Horse Is Us." *Newsweek*. Newsweek, 1 July 2008. Web. 12 Dec. 2013.

DIGITAL BOOKS, ARCHIVES, AND GOVERNMENT PUBLICATIONS

68. E-book on Kindle, iPad, or another device

Morrison, Toni. *Home*. New York: Vintage, 2013. Kindle file.

69. Document within an archive on the Web

Give the print information, then the title of the scholarly project or archive in italics, the medium of publication (*Web*), and the date of access (day, month, and year).

"New York Quiet." *Franklin Repository* 5 Aug. 1863, 1. *Valley of the Shadow*. Web. 23 Feb. 2014.

70. Government publication

If you cannot locate the author of the document, give the name of the government and the agency that published it.

United States. Dept. of Health and Human Services. *Salmonellosis Outbreak in Certain Types of Tomatoes*. US Dept. of Health and Human Services, 5 July 2008. Web. 30 Nov. 2013.

UNEDITED ONLINE SOURCES

71. Posting on social media

Many organizations now use *Facebook* and other social media. Give the author, title, name of the organization, the name of the site (e.g., *Facebook*), the date, the medium (*Web*), and the date of access.

Eklund, Doug. "Dedicated to Myself." *Metropolitan Museum of Art. Facebook*, 14 Mar. 2013. Web. 18 Mar. 2013.

72. Posting on *Twitter*

Include the entire tweet and the time of publication. Conclude with the medium (*Tweet*).

Obama, Barack (BO). "It should not be a partisan issue." Utah business leaders urge their representative to move on #immigration reform. 27 Aug. 2013. 12:02 p.m. Tweet.

73. Wiki entry

Wiki content is written collaboratively, thus no author is listed. Because the content on a wiki changes frequently, wikis are not considered reliable scholarly sources.

"Snowboard." *Wikipedia*. Wikimedia Foundation, 2014. Web. 30 Jan. 2014.

74. E-mail and text messaging

Give the name of the writer, the subject line, a description of the message, the date, and the medium of delivery (*E-mail, Text message*).

Ballmer, Steve. "A New Era of Business Productivity and Innovation." Message to Microsoft Executive E-mail. 30 Nov. 2006. E-mail.

75. Posting to a discussion list

Give the name of the writer, the subject line, the name of the list in italics, the publisher, the date of the posting, the medium (*Web*), and the date of access.

Dobrin, Sid. "Re: ecocomposition?" *Writing Program Administration*. Arizona State U, 19 Dec. 2008. Web. 5 Jan. 2014.

76. Course home page

Sparks, Julie. "English Composition 1B." Course home page. San Jose State U, Fall 2013. Web. 17 Sept. 2013.

77. Blog entry

If there is no sponsor or publisher for the blog, use *N.p.*

Arrington, Michael. "Think Before You Voicemail." *TechCrunch*. N.p., 5 July 2008. Web. 10 Sept. 2013.

14i Visual Sources

78. Cartoon or comic strip

Trudeau, G. B. "Doonesbury." Comic strip. *Washington Post* 21 Apr. 2008. C15. Print.

79. Advertisement

Begin with the name of the advertiser or product, then the word *Advertisement.*

Nike. Advertisement. ABC. 8 Oct. 2010. Television.

80. Map, graph, or chart

Specify *Map, Graph,* or *Chart* after the title.

Greenland. Map. Vancouver: International Travel Maps, 2004. Print.

VISUAL SOURCES ON THE WEB

81. Photograph on the Web

Include the photographer, title of the image, and the date, then the name of the Web site, the medium (*Web*), and the date of access.

Swansburg, John. *The Illinois Monument at the Vicksburg National Military Park.* 2010. *Slate.com.* Web. 18 Oct. 2013.

82. Photograph from an archive

Include the photographer, title of the image, the name of the archive, the medium (*Web*), and the date of access.

Parks, Gordon. *Washington, D.C. Government Charwoman.* 1942. Prints and Photographs Div., Lib. of Cong. *America from the Great Depression to World War II: Photographs from the FSA-OWI, 1935-1945.* Web. 23 Oct. 2013.

83. Video on the Web

Video on the Web often lacks a creator and a date. Begin the entry with a title if you cannot find a creator. Use *n.d.* if you cannot find a date.

Wesch, Michael. *A Vision of Students Today. YouTube.* YouTube, 2007. Web. 28 May 2013.

84. Work of art on the Web

Include the artist, title of the work in italics, and the date. For works found on the Web, omit the medium but include the location or museum, then add the name of the Web site, the medium (*Web*), and the date of access.

Mapplethorpe, Robert. *Self-Portrait.* 1972. Palm Springs Art Museum. *Robert Mapplethorpe Foundation*, n.d. Web. 3 Nov. 2013.

85. Map on the Web

"Lansing, Michigan." Map. *Google Maps*. Google, 2014. Web. 19 Nov. 2014.

86. Cartoon or comic strip on the Web

Tomorrow, Tom. "Modern World." Comic strip. *Huffington Post*. HuffingtonPost.com, 2 Jan. 2014. Web. 20 Jan. 2014.

14j Multimedia Sources

87. Podcast

Sussingham, Robin. "All Things Autumn." No. 2. *HighLifeUtah*. N.p., 20 Nov. 2006. Web. 28 Feb. 2014.

88. Film

Begin with the title in italics. List the director, the distributor, the date, and the medium. Other data, such as the names of the screenwriters and performers, are optional.

Wanted. Dir. Timur Bekmambetov. Perf. James McAvoy, Angelina Jolie, and Morgan Freeman. Universal, 2008. Film.

89. DVD

No Country for Old Men. Dir. Joel Coen and Ethan Coen. Perf. Tommy Lee Jones, Javier Bardem, and Josh Brolin. Paramount, 2007. DVD.

90. Television or radio program

"Kaisha." *The Sopranos*. Perf. James Gandolfini, Lorraine Bracco, and Edie Falco. HBO. 4 June 2006. Television.

91. Telephone interview

Zuckerberg, Mark. Telephone interview. 5 Mar. 2013.

92. **Speech, debate, mediated discussion, or public talk**

> Clinton, Hillary Rodham. "Frontllines and Frontiers: Making Human Rights a Human Reality." Dublin City U. Ireland. 6 Dec. 2012. Address.

Sample Research Paper with MLA Documentation

FORMATTING A RESEARCH PAPER IN MLA STYLE

MLA offers these general guidelines for formatting a research paper.

- **Use white, 8½-by-11-inch paper.** Don't use colored or lined paper.
- **Double-space everything—the title, headings, body of the paper, quotations, and works-cited list.** Set the line spacing on your word processor for double-spacing and leave it there.
- **Put your last name and the page number at the top of every page, aligned with the right margin, ½ inch from the top of the page.** Your word processor has a header command that will automatically put a header with the page number on every page.
- **Specify 1-inch margins.** One-inch margins are the default setting for most word processors.
- **Do not justify (make even) the right margin.** Justifying the right margin throws off the spacing between words and makes your paper harder to read. Use the left-align setting instead.
- **Indent the first line of each paragraph ½ inch (five spaces).** Set the paragraph indent command or the tab on the ruler of your word processor at ½ inch.
- **Use the same readable typeface throughout your paper.** Use a standard typeface such as Times New Roman, 12 point.
- **Use block format for quotations longer than four lines.** See pages 105–106.
- **MLA does not require a title page.** Unless your instructor asks for a separate title page, put 1 inch from the top of the page to your name, your instructor's name, the course, and the date (on separate lines). Center your title on the next line. Do not underline your title or put it inside quotation marks.

1"

1/2"

Lopez 1

Include your last name and page number as page header, beginning with the first page, 1/2" from the top.

MLA style does not require a title page. Check with your instructor to find out whether you need one.

Gabriella Lopez

Professor Kimbro

English 1102

6 May 2013

Establishing a Campus Garden

Center the title. Do not underline the title; put it inside quotation marks or type it in all capital letters.

1/2"

1"

When high school seniors begin to look at colleges and universities, they consider many factors: location, academics, and the quality of campus life, including food service. Now prospective students are also considering sustainability. According to a 2006 article in *USA Today*, students are increasingly interested in schools with "green" practices, which offer local, sustainable, and organic options in their food service (Horovitz). In 2009, the *Princeton Review* found that 66% of high school-age college applicants and parents surveyed "would find information about a college's dedication to the environment useful in their college selection process" (Klinck).

Do not include a page number for items without pagination, such as Web sites.

Specify 1" margins all around. Double-space everything.

Higher education is responding. Colleges and universities lead other institutions and industries with 3,850 LEED (Leadership in Energy and Environmental Design) certified buildings (Klinck), and show commitment to recycling and waste-reduction programs. Furthermore, schools are increasingly devoting at least a portion of food budgets to buying from local farms and producers (Pino). And this trend should only grow: the 2009-2014 Strategic Plan of the National Association of College and University Food Service (NACUFS) calls for the organization to become an integral player in sustainability policy-making and programming for higher education by advocating for and

1"

1"

Lopez 2

providing education on sustainable food service policies and practices. Some schools, most notably Yale University, have even established farms and gardens on or near campus that serve as living classrooms for environmental studies and provide food for students as well as the community (Samadzadeh).

Indent each paragraph five spaces (1/2" on the ruler in your word processor).

"Going green" is not easy, nor is it inexpensive. For those reasons, many schools, including our own, are finding it difficult to move beyond campus-wide recycling programs to other initiatives such as increasing the amount of local organic foods in the dining halls. The fact that many colleges contract with outside food service vendors makes this goal even more difficult. An alternative approach, however, can provide both fresh, healthy food and hands-on experience in environmental stewardship. Establishing a small organic campus garden is a low-cost, high-yield way to support our school's mission, our students, the local community, and the global environment.

Lopez's thesis appears here, at the end of her third paragraph.

Our school in particular has a stated commitment to creating a campus in which students feel safe and sustained in an environment that is, according to the Web page, "contingent on the everyday learning process." One of the immediate benefits to establishing a campus organic garden is promoting a healthy relationship to food. According to a survey of 2,200 American college students, a significant number of women and a smaller group of men have "major concerns about eating and food with respect to both weight and health" (Rozin, Bauer, and Catanese 132). The negative feelings about food that result from these concerns can lead to eating disorders, primarily in

Give page numbers for paraphrases as well as direct quotations.

Lopez 3

young women (140). In short, Americans have become neurotic about eating. Michael Pollan attributes this anxiety to "nutritionism": the belief, fueled by food scientists and the food industry, that nutrients and the energy (or calorie) count is more important than actual food, and since nutrients exist at the molecular level, we believe we need to eat "scientifically," under the direction of the experts (8). This promotion of discrete nutrients over whole food has led to the industrialization of food production—more processed foods, more artificial grains, more chemicals to raise animals and vegetables in vast "monocultures," more sugars and fats, and less variety in our diet that has been reduced to a glut of wheat, corn, and soy (10). Thus, not only is our industrialized diet making us physically sick; in fact, it is also making us emotionally unhealthy. Pollan observes that food concerns much more than nutrition: "Food is all about pleasure, about community, about family and spirituality, about our relationship to the natural world, and about expressing our identity"(8).

Use a signal phrase to include the author's name before a quotation from a source.

Colleges are becoming increasingly aware of the relationships among individual, social, and environmental health, and that projects like campus farms and gardens serve not only students, but also the local population, and even the planet (Pino). The Dartmouth Organic Farm Web site points to these connections:

Lopez introduces the block quotation, naming the source in the text.

> The very nature of an agricultural enterprise lies in the intersection of culture and the environment, to identify and respond to the needs of a society while

Lopez 4

Quotations of more than four lines should be indented 1" or ten spaces. Do not use quotation marks.

> recognizing the limits and demands of the immediate, local ecosystem. A farm is one of the last institutionalized vestiges of our direct connection to the natural world that surrounds and supports us.

There is evidence to support these claims. A study in the United Kingdom found that people with the highest levels of "ecoliteracy" (accumulated ecological knowledge) acquired that knowledge through direct experience and talking with others rather than from schooling and television (Pilgrim, Smith, and Pretty).

One of the missions of our school, as stated on our Web site, is "the development of men and women dedicated to the service of others." Establishing a campus organic farm that could immediately serve as a model of sound nutritional and environmental practices, and perhaps one day provide food for local relief organizations, certainly supports this mission.

Another benefit to establishing a campus organic garden is that it would provide educational opportunities to students who are interested in the growing field of sustainability. As concern about the environment grows, colleges and universities are beginning to incorporate sustainability into their programs. Environmental studies classes and majors are growing and diversifying. Students can now get MBAs in sustainable-business practices and train to build and operate wind turbines, among other things (Berman). In the area of public policy, a major in this field is also becoming more valuable. The *New York*

Lopez 5

Sources not identified with an author are referenced by a shortened title.

Times Magazine notes this cultural trend: "Time was, environmental-studies majors ran campus recycling programs. Now they run national campaigns" ("Learn").

Because our school is much smaller and has fewer resources than Yale or most of the other schools with well-known and successful sustainable food projects, including Dartmouth, Rutgers, Dickinson, Boston College, Colby, Columbia, Wisconsin-Madison, Iowa State, UCSD (University of California, San Diego), UCLA, and the University of Nebraska, establishing a farm or a large garden seems improbable. I propose that we establish a campus garden following the very simple principles of organic "square-foot" gardening. Square-foot gardening is raised-bed gardening that takes place in 6- to 12-inch-deep frames that have been segmented into a grid (see fig. 1). The size of each square in the grid depends on what plants are planted there; certain plants require larger and deeper grids (Bartholomew 15-16). The main benefit of square-foot gardening is that one can grow the same amount of

Position figures close to the text where they are mentioned. Include a figure number followed by a caption.

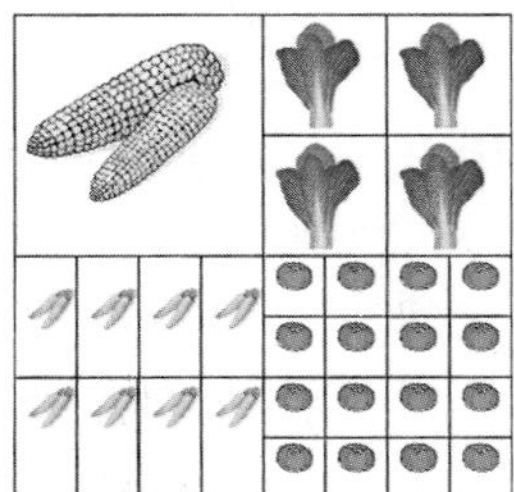

Fig. 1. The grid in a square-foot gardening plot is divided according to the mature size of each plant.

Because Lopez illustrates the point with a figure she created, no source information is needed.

Lopez 6

produce in a 140-square-foot grid that is typically grown in the average 700-square-foot, single-row garden (42). Thus, a garden—or multiple gardens, placed strategically according to the sunlight needs of the plants—can be fitted into small spaces around campus.

Another great benefit to the square-foot garden is that the smaller beds are easily adapted to grow seasonal crops, making it easier to recognize and explore the foods within our foodshed, or regional food chain, as the locavore movement encourages ("Why"). The smaller size of the beds also means that crops and harvests can be staggered. Regular row planting replicates the same kinds of yields as industrial farming, meaning that an entire row of the same item is harvested all at once, which can lead to waste. Staggering crops ensures that only what is needed is grown and harvested (18), and staggering maximizes use of the space. In short, square-foot gardening is ideal for a small group of beginning gardeners (13). In addition, it is easy to modify as need and skill level dictates, as amateur gardeners show in their *YouTube* videos (see, for example, mokahdeelyte).

Lopez mentions a *YouTube* video and parenthetical reference leads to entry in Works Cited list.

Even though our campus organic garden will not be built on the same scale as at the larger schools, much can still be learned from them, especially regarding how they gain support and how they maintain interest in their project. The key to both Yale's Sustainable Food Project and Dartmouth's Organic Farm is activist students. Unlike student activists of the past, however, today's students are working with school administrators to make change

Lopez 7

possible. And school administrators are seeing the surge in green activism on campus as something that could appeal to prospective freshmen and alumni alike (Lewington). Establishing a core group of students responsible for shepherding the project is essential; these students can then start finding allies on campus. Other successful activist student groups are a good possibility, as are like-minded faculty, and food service administration and staff.

Cite publications within the text by the name of the author (or authors).

Once support is gained from students, faculty, staff, and administration, the logistics of building the gardens can get under way. Little space and few resources and tools are necessary for square-foot gardening but supplies such as building materials, ingredients for the soil mixture, and seeds will still have to be gathered. Compost for the soil mixture can be made from existing kitchen waste. Seeds, peat moss, vermiculite, and small tools are not expensive and can be bought with donated funds. Partnering with a community organic gardening organization or individuals in the community may not only yield donated or discounted supplies but also training for student volunteers and a tie to the local community, which can help maintain support for the project in the long term.

Maintaining interest is important to keeping support, getting volunteer labor, and allowing for future growth. Holding events is one way to keep the excitement going. Yale's Sustainable Food Project offers cooking classes, uses a pizza oven installed on the farm to bake pizzas every Friday to thank volunteers, and even hosts an annual pig roast to celebrate the end of

Lopez uses sources to show how her proposal has worked for other campuses.

Lopez 8

classes (Samadzadeh). Events of this scale are probably not an option for a smaller garden, but working with food service to create theme menus, such as Colby's "Garlic Fest," can attract attention (Jacobs). In addition, highlighting the farm or garden during student orientation and during parent weekends not only helps garner financial support but also attracts new volunteers.

The conclusion uses a quotation that appeals to readers' values and repeats call to action.

As sustainability becomes increasingly important in society, colleges and universities have increased responsibility not only to be models of sustainable practices, but also to train students for jobs in an economy and environment informed by sustainability. The Sustainable Endowments Institute urges, "Colleges and universities, as leaders of innovation in our society, have the potential to demonstrate sustainable principles in their campus operations and endowment policies. Their examples can provide a road map for others to follow" ("Frequently"). For our college to remain competitive with other schools, we need to increase our commitment to these important ideas. Establishing a campus garden should be the first step.

Lopez 9

Works Cited

Center "Works Cited" on a new page.

Bartholomew, Mel. *All New Square Foot Gardening: Grow More in Less Space*. Franklin: Cool Spring P, 2006. Print.

Berman, Jillian. "Sustainability Could Secure a Good Future: College Students Flock to 'Green' Degrees, Careers." *USA Today* 3 Apr. 2009, final ed.: 7D. *LexisNexis Academic*. Web. 6 Apr. 2013.

"Dartmouth Organic Farm." *Dartmouth Outdoor Club*. Dartmouth Coll., n.d. Web. 5 Apr. 2013.

"Frequently Asked Questions." *The College Sustainability Report Card*. Sustainable Endowments Institute, n.d. Web. 2 Apr. 2013.

Horovitz, Bruce. "More University Students Call for Organic, 'Sustainable' Food." *USA Today*. USA Today, 26 Sept. 2006. Web. 2 Apr. 2013.

Jacobs, Ruth. "Organic Garden Gives Back." *Colby Magazine* 99.1 (2010): n. pag. Web. 2 Apr. 2013.

Klinck, Betty. "Find a Green College: Check! Princeton Review Helps Applicants Who Seek Sustainability." *USA Today* 20 Apr. 2010, final ed.: 7D. *LexisNexis Academic*. Web. 20 Apr. 2013.

"Learn," *New York Times Magazine* 20 Apr. 2008: 61. *LexisNexis Academic*. Web. 2 Apr. 2013.

Lewington, Jennifer. "Lean Green Campus Machines: Students Are at the Forefront of a Grassroots Environmental Revolution as They Coax—and Sometimes Embarrass—Administrators into Walking the Walk with Them." *Globe and Mail* [Toronto] 23 Oct. 2008: 14. *LexisNexis Academic*. Web. 8 Apr. 2013.

Double-space all entries. Indent all but the first line in each entry 1/2".

If the date of publication is not available, use the abbreviation *n.d.*

Alphabetize entries by the last names of the authors or by the first important word in the title if no author is listed.

When the city of publication is not included in the name of a newspaper, add the city name in brackets after the name of the newspaper.

Lopez 10

List the title of videos or films in italics if the work is independent. Include in quotation marks if it is part of a larger work.

mokahdeelyte. *Square Foot Gardening Modified Tutorial. YouTube.* YouTube, 17 May 2008. Web. 3 Apr. 2013.

NACUFS. "Strategic Plan, 2009-2014." *NACUFS*. Natl. Assn. of Coll. and Univ. Food Services, n.d. Web. 5 Apr. 2013.

Journal article

Pilgrim, Sarah, David Smith, and Jules Pretty. "A Cross-Regional Assessment of the Factors Affecting Ecoliteracy: Implications for Policy and Practice." *Ecological Applications* 17.6 (2007): 1742-51. Print.

Pino, Carl. "Sustainability on the Menu: College Cafeterias Are Buying Local and Going Organic." *E-Magazine.com*. E-The Environmental Magazine, Mar./Apr. 2008. Web. 3 Apr. 2013.

Book

Pollan, Michael. *In Defense of Food: An Eater's Manifesto*. New York: Penguin, 2008. Print.

Journal article from a database

Rozin, Paul, Rebecca Bauer, and Dana Catanese. "Food and Life, Pleasure and Worry, Among American College Students: Gender Differences and Regional Similarities." *Journal of Personality and Social Psychology* 85.1 (2003): 132-41. *PsycARTICLES*. Web. 6 Apr. 2013.

Blog entry

Samadzadeh, Nozlee. "Farm Update: The Third Annual Jack Hitt Annual Last Day of Classes Pig Roast." *Yale Sustainable Food Project Student Blog*. Yale Sustainable Food Project, 3 May 2010. Web. 5 Apr. 2013.

Go through your text and make sure all the sources you have used are in the list of works cited.

"Why Eat Locally?" *Locavore*. Locavores, n.d. Web. 6 Apr. 2013.

FORMATTING THE WORKS CITED IN MLA STYLE

- **Begin the works-cited list on a new page.** Insert a page break with your word processor before you start the works-cited page.
- **Center "Works Cited" on the first line at the top of the page.**
- **Double-space all entries.**
- **Alphabetize each entry by the last name of the author or, if no author is listed, by the first content word in the title (ignore *a, an, the*).**
- **Indent all but the first line in each entry ½ inch.**
- **Italicize the titles of books and periodicals.**
- **If an author has more than one entry, list the entries in alphabetical order by title. Use three hyphens in place of the author's name for the second and subsequent entries.**

  Murphy, Dervla. *Cameroon with Egbert*. Woodstock: Overlook, 1990. Print.

  ---. *Full Tilt: Ireland to India with a Bicycle*. London: Murray, 1965. Print.

- **Go through your paper to check that each source you have used is in the works-cited list.**

15 APA Documentation

QUICK*TAKE*

- Use in-text citations in APA style (see pp. 116–119)
- Create citations for print sources (see pp. 127–129)
- Create citations for online sources (see pp. 130–132)

APA DOCUMENTATION MAP

1 Collect the right information

For every source you need to have

- the name of the author or authors,
- the full title, and
- complete publication information.

For instructions go to the illustrated examples in Section 15b of the four major source types:

- **PERIODICAL SOURCES**
- **BOOKS AND NONPERIODICAL SOURCES**
- **ONLINE SOURCES**

For other kinds of sources such as visual and multimedia sources, see the Index of References on p. 126.

2 Cite sources in two places

Remember, this is a two-part process.

To create citations

(a) in **the body of your paper**, go to 15a.

(b) in a **list of References at the end of your paper**, go to 15b.

Social sciences disciplines—including government, linguistics, psychology, sociology, and education—frequently use the American Psychological Association (APA) documentation style. The APA style is similar to the MLA style in many ways. Both styles use parenthetical citations in the body of the text, with complete bibliographical citations in the list of references at the end. Both styles avoid using footnotes for references.

If you have questions that the examples in this chapter do not address, consult the *Publication Manual of the American Psychological Association*, sixth edition (2010).

3 Find the right model citations

You'll find **illustrated examples of sources** in 15b.

Once you match your source to one of those examples, you can move on to more specific examples:

- **PERIODICAL SOURCES,** go to 15c.
- **BOOKS AND NONPERIODICAL SOURCES**, go to 15d.
- **ONLINE SOURCES**, go to 15e.

A complete list of examples is found in the Index of References on p. 126.

4 Format your paper

You will find pages from a **sample research paper in APA style** in 15g.

A note about footnotes:

APA style does not use footnotes for documentation. Use in-text citations instead (see 15a).

15a In-text Citations in APA Style

APA style emphasizes the date of publication. When you cite an author's name, always follow it with the date of publication.

> Zukin (2004) observes that teens today begin to shop for themselves at age 13 or 14, "the same age when lower-class children, in the past, became apprentices or went to work in factories" (p. 50).

If the author's name is not mentioned in the sentence, the reference looks like this:

> One sociologist notes that teens today begin to shop for themselves at age 13 or 14, "the same age when lower-class children, in the past, became apprentices or went to work in factories" (Zukin, 2004, p. 50).

The corresponding entry in the references list would be

> Zukin, S. (2004). *Point of purchase: How shopping changed American culture.* New York, NY: Routledge.

Paraphrase, summary, or short quotation

In APA style a short quotation has fewer than forty words.

> "The appeal of a shopping spree," one sociologist comments, "is not that you'll buy a lot of stuff; the appeal is that, among all the stuff you buy, you'll find what you truly desire" (Zukin, 2004, p. 112).

The author's name is provided in the parenthetical reference.

Quotations 40 words or longer

Orlean (2001) has attempted to explain the popularity of the painter Thomas Kinkade:

> People like to own things they think are valuable. . . . The high price of limited editions is part of their appeal; it implies that they are choice and exclusive, and that only a certain class of people will be able to afford them. (p. 128)

The sentence introducing the quotation names the author.

Note that the period appears before the parentheses in an indented "block" quote.

The date appears in parentheses immediately following the author's name.

Index of in-text citations

Sample in-text citations

1. Author named in your text

The influential sociologist Daniel Bell (1973) noted a shift in the United States to the "postindustrial society" (p. 3).

2. Author not named in your text

In 2012, the Gallup poll reported that 56% of adults in the United States think secondhand smoke is "very harmful," compared with only 36% in 1994 (Saad, 2013, p. 4).

3. Work by a single author

(Bell, 1973, p. 3)

4. Work by two authors

List both authors' last names, joined with an ampersand.

(Suzuki & Irabu, 2013, p. 404)

5. Work by three to five authors

The authors' last names follow the order of the title page.

(Francisco, Vaughn, & Romano, 2012, p. 7)

Subsequent references can use the first author's name and *et al.*

(Francisco et al., 2012, p. 17)

6. Work by six or more authors

Use the first author's last name and *et al.* for all in-text references.

(Swallit et al., 2014, p. 49)

7. Work by a group or organization

Identify the group in the text and place the page number in parentheses.

The National Organization for Women (2001) observed that this "generational shift in attitudes toward marriage and childrearing" will have profound consequences (p. 325).

8. Work by an unknown author

Use a shortened version of the title (or the full title if it is short) in place of the author's name. Capitalize all key words in the title. If it is an article title, place it inside quotation marks.

> ("Derailing the Peace Process," 2014, p. 44)

9. Two works by one author published in the same year

Assign the dates letters (*a*, *b*, etc.) according to their alphabetical arrangement in the references list.

> The majority of books written about coauthorship focus on partners of the same sex (Laird, 2007a, p. 351).

10. Digital source

If an online or other digital source does not provide page numbers, use the paragraph number preceded by the abbreviation *para.*

> (Robinson, 2014, para. 7)

11. Two or more sources within the same sentence

Place each citation directly after the statement it supports.

> Some surveys report an increase in homelessness rates (Alford, 2004), while others chart a slight decrease (Rice, 2006a) . . .

If you need to cite two or more works within the same parentheses, list them in the order in which they appear in the References list.

> (Alford, 2004; Rice, 2006a)

12. Work cited in another source

> Saunders and Kellman's study (as cited in Rice, 2006a)

15b Illustrated Samples and Index of References Entries in APA Style

Periodical Sources

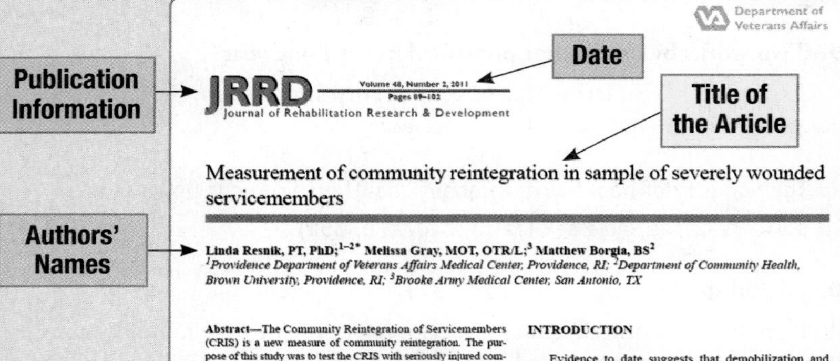

JRRD Journal of Rehabilitation Research & Development

Volume 48, Number 2, 2011
Pages 89–102

Measurement of community reintegration in sample of severely wounded servicemembers

Linda Resnik, PT, PhD;[1–2*] Melissa Gray, MOT, OTR/L;[3] Matthew Borgia, BS[2]
[1]Providence Department of Veterans Affairs Medical Center, Providence, RI; [2]Department of Community Health, Brown University, Providence, RI; [3]Brooke Army Medical Center, San Antonio, TX

Abstract—The Community Reintegration of Servicemembers (CRIS) is a new measure of community reintegration. The purpose of this study was to test the CRIS with seriously injured combat veterans. Subjects were 68 patients at the Center for the Intrepid. Each patient completed three CRIS subscales, the 36-Item Short Form Health Survey for Veterans (SF-36V), the Quality of Life Scale (QOLS), and two Craig Handicap Assessment and Reporting Technique subscales at visit 1 and the 3-month follow-up. Of the patients, 11 also completed the measures within 2 weeks of visit 1. We abstracted diagnoses and activities of daily living from the medical record. We evaluated test-retest reliability using intraclass correlation coefficients (ICCs). We evaluated concurrent validity with Pearson product moment correlations. We used multivariate analyses of variance to compare scores for subjects with and without posttraumatic stress disorder (PTSD), traumatic brain injury (TBI), and depression. Responsiveness analyses evaluated floor and ceiling effects, percent achieving minimal detectable change (MDC), effect size (ES), and the standardized response mean (SRM). CRIS subscale ICCs were 0.90 to 0.91. All subscales were moderately or strongly correlated with QOLS and SF-36V subscales. CRIS subscale scores were lower in PTSD and TBI groups ($p < 0.05$). CRIS Extent of Participation and Satisfaction with Participation subscales were lower for subjects with depression ($p < 0.05$). Of the sample, 17.4% to 23.2% had change greater than MDC. The ES ranged from 0.227 to 0.273 (SRM = 0.277–0.370), showing a small effect between visit 1 and the 3-month follow-up. Results suggest that the CRIS is a psychometrically sound choice for community reintegration measurement in severely wounded servicemembers.

Key words: community reintegration, disability, measurement, military healthcare, outcomes assessment, participation, psychometric testing, reliability, traumatic brain injury, veterans.

INTRODUCTION

Evidence to date suggests that demobilization and return home after combat can be challenging for military servicemembers. Numerous reintegration problems have been reported among veterans from the gulf war and more recent conflicts in Iraq and Afghanistan, including marital difficulties, financial difficulties, problems with alcohol or substance abuse, medical problems, behavioral problems such as depression or anxiety [1], homelessness [2], and motor vehicle accidents [3]. Readjustment to

Abbreviations: ADL = activity of daily living, ANOVA = analysis of variance, BAMC = Brooke Army Medical Center, CFI = Center for the Intrepid, CHART = Craig Handicap Assessment and Reporting Technique, CRIS = Community Reintegration of Servicemembers, ES = effect size, ICC = intraclass correlation coefficient, ICF = International Classification of Function, IED = improvised explosive device, MANOVA = multivariate analysis of variance, MDC = minimal detectable change, OEF = Operation Enduring Freedom, OIF = Operation Iraqi Freedom, PF-10 = 10-Item Physical Functioning Subscale, PTSD = posttraumatic stress disorder, QOLS = Quality of Life Scale, SD = standard deviation, SF-36V = 36-Item Short Form Health Survey for Veterans, SRM = standardized response mean, TBI = traumatic brain injury, VA = Department of Veterans Affairs.

*Address all correspondence to Linda Resnik, PT, PhD; Providence VA Medical Center, 830 Chalkstone Ave, Providence, RI 02908; 401-273-7100, ext 2368; fax: 401-863-3489. **Email:** Linda_Resnik@brown.edu

DOI:10.1682/JRRD.2010.04.0070

Resnik, L., Gray, M., & Borgia, M. (2011). "Measurement of community reintegration in sample of severely wounded servicemembers." *Journal of Rehabilitation Research & Development 48*(2), 89–102. http://dx.doi.org/10.1682/JRRD.2010.04.0070

Elements of the citation

Author's Name

The author's last name comes first, followed by the author's initials.

Join two authors' names with a comma and an ampersand.

Date of Publication

Give the year the work was published in parentheses.

Newspapers and popular magazines are referenced by the year, month, and day of publication.

Title of Article

- Do not use quotation marks. If there is a book title in the article title, italicize it.
- Titles of articles in APA style follow standard sentence capitalization.

Publication Information

Name of journal

- Italicize the journal name.
- Put a comma after the journal name.

Volume, issue, and page numbers

- Italicize the volume number.
- If each issue of the journal begins on page 1, give the issue number in parentheses, followed by a comma.
- If the article has been assigned a DOI (Digital Object Identifier), list it as a URL after the page numbers but without a period at the end.

Find the right example for your model (you may need to refer to more than one model)

What type of article do you have?

A scholarly journal article or abstract?

- For an article in a journal with continuous pagination, go to page 127, #17.
- For an article in a journal paginated by issue, go to page 127, #18.

A newspaper article?

- For a newspaper article, go to page 128, #20.

How many authors are listed?

- One, two, or more authors: go to page 127, #13–15.
- Unknown author: go to page 127, #16.

Books and Nonperiodical Sources

Title of Book

FIVE MINDS FOR THE

FUTURE

Author Name

Howard Gardner

HARVARD BUSINESS SCHOOL PRESS

BOSTON, MASSACHUSETTS

Publisher and Place of Publication

Gardner, H. (2007). *Five minds for the future.* Boston, MA: Harvard Business School Press.

Elements of the citation

Author's or Editor's Name

The author's last name comes first, followed by a comma and the author's initials.

If there is an editor, put the abbreviation *Ed*. in parentheses after the name. **Kavanagh, P. (Ed.).**

Year of Publication

- Give the year the work was copyrighted in parentheses.
- If no copyright year is given, write *n.d.* ("no date") in parentheses.

Book Title

- Italicize the title.
- Titles of books in APA style follow standard sentence capitalization: Capitalize only the first word, proper nouns, and the first word after a colon.

Publication Information

Place of publication

- For all books, list the city with a two-letter state abbreviation (or full country name) after the city name.
- If more than one city is given on the title page, list only the first.

Publisher's name

Do not shorten or abbreviate words like *University* and *Press*. Omit words such as *Co.*, *Inc.*, and *Publishers*.

Find the right example for your model (you may need to refer to more than one model)

How many authors are listed?

One, two, or more authors: go to pages 128–129, #21–24.

Do you have only a part of a book?

- For a chapter in an edited collection, go to page 129, #25.
- For an article in a reference work, go to page 129, #26.

Do you have an e-book?

- For an e-book with a DOI, go to page 129, #28.
- For an e-book with no DOI assigned, go to page 129, #29.

Online Sources

Tenenbaum, D. J. (2005). Global warming: Arctic climate: The heat is on. *Environmental Health Perspectives, 113*, A91. http://dx.doi.org/10.1289/ehp.113-a91a

Elements of the citation

Author's Name or Organization

- Authorship is sometimes hard to discern for online sources. if you do have an author or creator to cite, follow the rules for periodicals and books.
- If the only authority you find is a group or organization, list its name as the author.

Dates

Give the date the site was produced or last revised (sometimes the copyright date) after the author.

Title of Page or Article

- Web sites are often made up of many separate pages or articles. Each page or article on a Web site may or may not have a title.

URL and DOI

- If the article has a DOI (Digital Object Identifier), give the DOI in numeric or URL form after the title.
- If the article does not have a DOI, copy the Web address exactly as it appears in your browser window. You can even copy and paste the address into your text for greater accuracy.
- Break a URL at the end of a line *before* a mark of punctuation. Do not insert a hyphen.

Find the right example for your model (you may need to refer to more than one model)

What kind of publication do you have?

- For a document from a database, go to page 130, #30.
- For an article with a DOI assigned, go to page 131, #35.
- For an article in a newspaper or magazine, go to page 131, #36.
- For a government publication, go to page 130, #34.

Do you have a source that is posted by an individual?

- For a social media page or a *Twitter* post, go to page 131, #37–38.
- For a blog, go to page 131, #39.
- For e-mail or text messaging, go to page 132, #41.

Index of References Entries

15c Periodical Sources 127

15d Book Sources 128

15e Online Sources 130

15f Visual and Multimedia Sources 132

15c Periodical Sources in APA-style References

13. Article by one author

Goolkasian, P. (2012). Research in visual pattern recognition: The enduring legacy of studies from the 1960s. *American Journal of Psychology, 125*, 155–163.

14. Article by two authors

McClelland, D., & Eismann, K. (2013).

15. Article by three or more authors

List last names and initials for up to seven authors, with an ampersand between the last two names. For works with eight or more authors, list the first six names, then an ellipsis, then the last author's name.

Andis, S., Franks, D., Gee, G., Ng, K., Orr, V., Ray, B., . . . Tate, L.

16. Article by an unknown author

The green gene revolution [Editorial]. (2004, February). *Scientific American, 291*, 8.

17. Article in a journal with continuous pagination

Include only the volume number and the year, not the issue number.

Engen, R., & Steen, S. (2000). The power to punish: Discretion and sentencing reform in the war on drugs. *American Journal of Sociology, 105*, 1357–1395.

18. Article in a journal paginated by issue

If each issue of the journal begins on page 1, give the issue number in parentheses (not italicized) after the volume number.

Bunyan, T. (2010). Just over the horizon—the surveillance society and the state in the EU. *Race and Class, 51*(3), 1–12.

19. Monthly publications

Barth, A. (2010, March). Brain science gets squishy. *Discover*, 11–12.

20. Newspaper article

Olsen, E. (2010, June 22). A campaign for M&Ms with a salty center? Sweet. *The New York Times*, p. B6.

15d Books in APA-style References

21. Book by one author

Gladwell, M. (2011). *Outliers: The story of success*. New York, NY: Back Bay Books.

If there is an editor, put the abbreviation *Ed.* in parentheses after the name.

Rasgon, N. L. (Ed.). (2006). *The effects of estrogen on brain function*. Baltimore, MD: Johns Hopkins University Press.

22. Two or more books by the same author

Arrange according to the date, with the earliest publication first.

Jules, R. (2003). *Internal memos and other classified documents*. London, England: Hutchinson.

Jules, R. (2004). *Derelict cabinet*. London, England: Corgi-Transworld.

23. Book by two authors

Hardt, M., & Negri, A. (2000). *Empire*. Cambridge, MA: Harvard University Press.

24. Book by three or more authors

List last names and initials for up to seven authors, with an ampersand between the last two names. For works with eight or more authors, list the first six names, then an ellipsis, then the last author's name.

Anders, K., Child, H., Davis, K., Logan, O., Orr, J., Ray, B., . . . Wood, G.

25. Chapter in an edited collection

Boyaton, D. (2010). Behaviorism and its effect upon learning in schools. In G. Goodman (Ed.), *The educational psychology reader: The art and science of how people learn* (pp. 49–66). New York, NY: Peter Lang.

26. Article in a reference work

Viscosity. (2001). In *The Columbia encyclopedia* (6th ed.). New York, NY: Columbia University Press.

27. Religious or classical texts

Reference entries are not required for major classical works or the Bible, but in the first in-text citation, identify the edition used.

John 3.16 (Modern Phrased Version)

28. E-book with DOI

Chaffe-Stengel, P., & Stengel, D. (2012). *Working with sample data: Exploration and inference.* http://dx.doi.org/10.4128/9781606492147

29. E-book with no DOI assigned

Burton, R. (1832). *The anatomy of melancholy.* Retrieved from http://etext.library.adelaide.edu.au/b/burton/robert/melancholy

15e Online Sources in APA-style References

30. Document from a database

APA no longer requires listing the names of well-known databases. Include the name of the database only for hard-to-find books and other items.

Holloway, J. D. (2004). Protecting practitioners' autonomy. *Monitor on Psychology, 35*(1), 30.

31. Abstract retrieved from a database

Putsis, W. P., & Bayus, B. L. (2001). An empirical analysis of firms' product line decisions. *Journal of Marketing Research, 37*(8), 110–118. Abstract retrieved from PsycINFO database.

32. Online publication by a known author

Carr, A. (2003, May 22). *AAUW applauds Senate support of title IX resolution*. Retrieved from http://www.aauw.org/about /newsroom/press_releases/030522.cfm

33. Online publication by a group or organization

Girls Inc. (2013). *Girls' bill of rights*. Retrieved from http://www .girlsinc.org/about/girls-bill-of-rights/

34. Online government publication

U.S. Public Health Service. Office of the Surgeon General. (2001, March 11). *Women and smoking*. Retrieved from http://www .surgeongeneral.gov/library/womenandtobacco/

In-text

(U.S. Public Health Service [USPHS], 2001)

35. Online article with DOI assigned

There is no need to list the database or the retrieval date if the DOI is listed.

> Erdfelder, E. (2008). Experimental psychology: Good news. *Experimental Psychology, 55*(1), 1–2. doi:0.1027 /1618–3169.55.1.1

36. Article in an online magazine or newspaper

> Resinkoff, N. (2010, June 22). Media ignores Gulf tragedy: Focuses on campaign narrative. *Salon*. Retrieved from http://www.salon.com

37. Social media (e.g. Facebook) page or note

> The Daily Show. (2013, March 18). Political speeches contain much more than empty promises. [Facebook page]. Retrieved July 29, 2013, from https://www.facebook.com/thedailyshow

38. *Twitter* update or tweet

> Collins, F. S. (2013, April 30). Check out my NPR interview this afternoon with Marketplace's @kairyssdal about #NIH research: https://bit.ly/uvvDF8 [Tweet]. Retrieved from https://twitter .com/NIH

39. Blog entry

> Spinuzzi, C. (2010, January 7). In the pipeline [Blog post]. Retrieved from http://spinuzzi.blogspot.com/search?updated -max=2010-01-25T12%3A35%3A00-06%3A00

40. Wiki

> Mount Everest. (n.d.). In *Wikipedia*. Retrieved November 12, 2013, from http://en.wikipedia.org/wiki/Mt._Everest

41. E-mail or text messaging

E-mail sent from one individual to another should be cited as a personal communication. Personal communication is cited in text but not included in the reference list.

(D. Jenkins, personal communication, July 28, 2014)

15f Visual and Multimedia Sources in APA-style References

42. Television program

Winter, T. (Writer), & Van Patten, T. (Director). (2012). Resolution [Television series episode]. In A. T. Winter (Producer), *Boardwalk empire*. New York, NY: HBO.

43. Film, Video, or DVD

Boal, M. (Writer), & Bigelow, K. (Director). (2012). *Zero dark thirty* [Motion picture]. United States: Columbia Pictures.

44. Audio or video file or podcast

Horne, E. (Producer). (2013, July 9). *Radiolab* [Audio podcast]. Retrieved from http://www.radiolab.org/series/podcasts/

45. Photograph or work of art

American Heart Association. (2009). *Hands-only CPR graphic* [Photograph]. Retrieved from http://handsonlycpr.org /assets/files/Hands-only%20me.pdf

46. Map, chart, or graph

Information Architects. (2010). Web trend map 4 [Map]. Retrieved from http://www.informationarchitects.jp/en/wtm4/

Sample Pages from a Research Paper with APA Documentation

Type the running head (the shortened title) for publication in all caps, flush left at the top.

Running head: OPPORTUNITIES FOR HIGH-SPEED RAIL 1

APA style uses a title page with a page number at the top right.

Opportunities for Developing High-Speed

Rail in the United States

Jacob J. Pietsch

The University of Texas at Austin

Center the title, name of author(s), and name of school.

Continue to use the running head with the page number in the top right.

OPPORTUNITIES FOR HIGH-SPEED RAIL 2

Abstract

Policymakers in the United States must consider the impact of continued population growth and corresponding freight requirements on underfunded transportation systems. Proactive investments in transportation systems such as high-speed rail provide these policymakers with an opportunity to build additional capacity to move people and freight. In light of public support for developing high-speed rail, careful investments in systems that will likely succeed can lead to deeper government investments in the future. Although policymakers may face political challenges in providing funding for high-speed rail, the need for transportation systems that can support population growth will only become more pressing over time.

Do not indent the first line of the abstract.

The abstract appears on a separate page with the title *Abstract*. An abstract may not exceed 150 words.

Double-space the abstract.

Give the full title at the beginning of the body of the report.

Specify 1" margins.

Indent each paragraph 1/2" on the ruler in the word processing program.

Opportunities for Developing High-Speed Rail in the United States

Many Americans may consider the limits of transportation systems only when they sit in traffic on their daily commutes, forgetting how easily they can access most modern conveniences thanks to previous generations' investments in highways, subways, ferries, light rail, railroads, and air systems. On the one hand, the networks of transportation that connect America's cities and weave them into the global economy have facilitated unprecedented economic growth; on the other, failing transportation systems have the potential to inhibit economic progress. As stress continues to build on America's current infrastructure, "the nation's roads, rails, ports, and airports will require huge new investments to accommodate an estimated 120 million additional Americans by 2050" (PennDesign, 2011, p. 199).

In addition to meeting the needs of a growing population, transportation systems must also carry material resources and commodities along an extensive transportation network. The Federal Railroad Administration estimates that for each American, freight transportation systems must carry "40 tons of freight . . . annually" (U.S. Department of Transportation, 2010, p. 4). The movement of people and goods places significant strain on the current transportation systems, most evident in phenomena such as traffic congestion and deteriorating roadways. A public relations consultant for Amtrak and Boeing, Joseph Vranich, points to the crux issue, "Every

References

Center *References.*

Benner, C., & Pastor, M. (2011). Moving on up? Regions, megaregions, and the changing geography of social equity organizing. *Urban Affairs Review, 47*(3), 315–348. doi:10.1177/1078087410391950

Button, K., & Reggiani, A. (2011). *Transportation and economic development challenges*. Retrieved from http://uar.sagepub.com/content/47/3/315.full.pdf

De Chant, T. (2011, May 27). U.S. not dense enough for high speed rail? Think again. Retrieved from http://persquaremile.com/2011/05/27/u-s-not-dense-enough-for-high-speed-rail-think-again/

Eisele, B., Schrank, D., & Lomax, T. (2011, September). *2011 congested corridors report*. Retrieved from the Texas Transportation Institute Web site: http://d2dtl5nnlpfr0r.cloudfront.net/tti.tamu.edu/documents/corridors-report-2011.pdf

Hagler, Y., & Todorovich, P. (2009, September). Where high speed rail works best. *America 2050*. Retrieved from http://www.america2050.org/pdf/2050_Report_Where_HSR_Works_Best.pdf

Kaderbeck, S., & Peterson, T. (1992). High-speed rail. *American City and County, 101*(11), 56.

PennDesign. (2011). *High-speed rail in the northeast megaregion: From vision to reality*. Retrieved from University of Pennsylvania School of Design Web site: http://www.design.upenn.edu/city-regional-planning/high-speed-rail-northeast-megaregion-vision-reality

Alphabetize entries by last name of the author.

Double-space all entries.

Indent all but the first line of each entry five spaces.

Go through your text and make sure that everything you have cited, except for personal communication, is in the list of references.

16 CMS Documentation

QUICK*TAKE*

- Use footnotes or endnotes for print sources in CMS style (see pp. 138–144)
- Use footnotes or endnotes for online sources in CMS style (see pp. 145–146)

Writers who publish in business, social sciences, fine arts, and humanities outside the discipline of English often use *The Chicago Manual of Style* (CMS) method of documentation. CMS guidelines allow writers a clear way of using footnotes and endnotes (rather than MLA and APA in-text citations) for citing the sources of quotations, summaries, and paraphrases. If you have questions after consulting this chapter, you can consult *The Chicago Manual of Style*, sixteenth edition (Chicago: University of Chicago Press, 2010), or visit the Web site (www.chicagomanualofstyle.org).

16a The Elements of CMS Documentation

CMS describes two systems of documentation, one similar to APA and the other a style that uses footnotes or endnotes, which is the focus of this chapter. In the footnote style, CMS uses a superscript number directly after any quotation, paraphrase, or summary. Notes are numbered consecutively throughout the essay, article, or chapter.

> In *Southern Honor: Ethics and Behavior in the Old South*, Wyatt-Brown argues that "paradox, irony, and guilt have been three current words used by historians to describe white Southern life before the Civil War."[1]

Note

> 1. Bertram Wyatt-Brown, *Southern Honor: Ethics and Behavior in the Old South* (Oxford: Oxford University Press, 1983), 3.

Bibliography

Wyatt-Brown, Bertram. *Southern Honor: Ethics and Behavior in the Old South*. Oxford: Oxford University Press, 1983.

Footnote and endnote placement

Footnotes appear at the bottom of the page on which each citation appears. Double-space footnotes and endnotes. **Endnotes** are compiled at the end of the text on a separate page, titled *Notes*.

CMS Bibliography

Because footnotes and endnotes in CMS format contain complete citation information, a separate list of references is often optional.

Index of CMS Documentation

16b Books and Nonperiodical Sources in CMS Style

Note

1. Nell Irvin Painter, *Creating Black Americans: African-American History and Its Meanings, 1619 to the Present* (New York: Oxford University Press, 2006), 5.

Bibliography

Painter, Nell Irvin. *Creating Black Americans: African-American History and Its Meanings, 1619 to the Present.* New York: Oxford University Press, 2006.

Author's or Editor's Name

In a note, the author's name is given in normal order.

In the bibliography, give the author's last name first. If there is an editor, put *ed*. after the name.

Book Title

Use the exact title, as it appears on the title page (not the cover).

Italicize the title.

Capitalize all nouns, verbs, adjectives, adverbs, and pronouns, and the first word of the title and subtitle.

Publication Information

In a note, the place of publication, publisher, and year of publication are in parentheses.

Place of publication

- Add the state's postal abbreviation or country when the city is not well known or ambiguous (*Cambridge, MA*, or *Cambridge, UK*).
- If more than one city is given on the title page, use the first.

Publisher's name

- You may use acceptable abbreviations (e.g., *Co*. for *Company*).

Year of publication

- If no year of publication is given, write *n.d.* ("no date") in place of the date.

Sample citations for books and nonperiodical sources

1. Book by one author

In a note, the author's name is given in normal order.

1. Thomas Friedman, *The World Is Flat: A Brief History of the Twenty-first Century* (New York: Farrar, Straus, and Giroux, 2005), 9.

In subsequent references, cite the author's last name only.

2. Friedman, 10.

If the reference is to the same work as the preceding note, you can use the abbreviation *Ibid.*:

3. Ibid., 10.

In the bibliography, give the author's name in reverse order.

Friedman, Thomas. *The World Is Flat: A Brief History of the Twenty-first Century*. New York: Farrar, Straus, and Giroux, 2005.

For edited books, put *ed.* after the name.

Chen, Kuan-Hsing, ed. *Trajectories: Inter-Asia Cultural Studies*. London: Routledge, 1998.

2. Book by multiple authors

For books with two or three authors, in a note, put all authors' names in normal order. (For subsequent references, give only the authors' last names.)

4. Taylor Hauser and June Kashpaw, *January Blues* (Foster City, CA: IDG Books, 2003), 32.

In the bibliography, give second and third names in normal order.

Hauser, Taylor, and June Kashpaw. *January Blues*. Foster City, CA: IDG Books, 2003.

When there are more than three authors, give the name of the first author listed, followed by *et al.* in a note. List all of the authors in the bibliography.

3. **Book by a group or organization**

Note

7. World Health Organization, *Advancing Safe Motherhood through Human Rights* (Geneva, Switzerland: World Health Organization, 2001), 18.

Bibliography

World Health Organization. *Advancing Safe Motherhood through Human Rights*. Geneva, Switzerland: World Health Organization, 2001.

4. **A selection in an anthology or a chapter in an edited collection**

Note

2. Renato Constantino, "Globalization and the South," in *Trajectories: Inter-Asia Cultural Studies*, ed. Kuan-Hsing Chen (London: Routledge, 1998), 57–64.

Bibliography

Constantino, Renato. "Globalization and the South." In *Trajectories: Inter-Asia Cultural Studies*, edited by Kuan-Hsing Chen, 57–64. London: Routledge, 1998.

5. Book with an editor

Note

1. Thomas Hardy, *Jude the Obscure*, ed. Norman Page (New York: Norton, 1999), 35.

Bibliography

Hardy, Thomas. *Jude the Obscure*. Edited by Norman Page. New York: Norton, 1999.

6. Government document

Note

5. US House Committee on Armed Services, *Comptroller General's Assessment of the Iraqi Government's Record of Performance* (Washington, DC: Government Printing Office, 2008), 40.

Bibliography

US House Committee on Armed Services. *Comptroller General's Assessment of the Iraqi Government's Record of Performance*. Washington, DC: Government Printing Office, 2008.

7. Religious texts

Citations from religious texts appear in the notes but not in the bibliography. Give the version in parentheses in the first citation only.

Note

4. John 3:16 (King James Version).

16c Periodical Sources in CMS Style

Note

1. Michael Hutt, "A Nepalese Triangle: Monarchists, Maoists, and Political Parties," *Asian Affairs* 38 (2007): 11–22.

Bibliography

Hutt, Michael. "A Nepalese Triangle: Monarchists, Maoists, and Political Parties." *Asian Affairs* 38 (2007): 11–22.

Author's or Editor's Name

In a note, the author's name is given in normal order.

In a bibliography, give the author's last name first.

Title of Article

- Put the title in quotation marks. If there is a title of a book within the title, italicize it.
- Capitalize nouns, verbs, adjectives, adverbs, and pronouns, and the first word of the title and subtitle.

Publication Information

Name of journal

- Italicize the name of the journal.
- Journal titles are normally not abbreviated in the arts and humanities unless the title of the journal is an abbreviation (*PMLA, ELH*).

Volume, issue, and page numbers

- Place the volume number after the journal title without intervening punctuation.
- For journals that are paginated from issue to issue within a volume, do not list the issue number.

Date

- The date or year of publication is given in parentheses after the volume number, or issue number, if provided.

Sample citations for periodical sources

8. Article by one author

Note

1. Sumit Guha, "Speaking Historically: The Changing Voices of Historical Narration in Western India, 1400–1900," *American Historical Review* 109 (2004): 1084–98.

Bibliography

Guha, Sumit. "Speaking Historically: The Changing Voices of Historical Narration in Western India, 1400–1900," *American Historical Review* 109 (2004): 1084–98.

9. Article by two or three authors

Note

3. Pamela R. Matthews and Mary Ann O'Farrell, "Introduction: Whose Body?" *South Central Review* 18, no. 3–4 (Fall–Winter 2001): 1–5.

Bibliography

Matthews, Pamela R., and Mary Ann O'Farrell. "Introduction: Whose Body?" *South Central Review* 18, no. 3–4 (Fall–Winter 2001): 1–5.

10. Article by more than three authors

Note

Give the name of the first listed author, followed by *et al.*

5. Michael J. Thompson et al., "The Internal Rotation of the Sun," *Annual Review of Astronomy and Astrophysics* 41 (2003): 602.

Bibliography

Thompson, Michael J., Jorgen Christensen-Dalsgaard, Mark S. Miesch, and Juri Toomre. "The Internal Rotation of the Sun." *Annual Review of Astronomy and Astrophysics* 41 (2003): 599–643.

11. **Journals paginated by volume**

Note

4. Susan Welsh, "Resistance Theory and Illegitimate Reproduction," *College Composition and Communication* 52 (2001): 553–73.

Bibliography

Welsh, Susan. "Resistance Theory and Illegitimate Reproduction." *College Composition and Communication* 52 (2001): 553–73.

12. **Journals paginated by issue**

Note

5. Tzvetan Todorov, "The New World Disorder," *South Central Review* 19, no. 2 (2002): 28–32.

Bibliography

Todorov, Tzvetan. "The New World Disorder." *South Central Review* 19, no. 2 (2002): 28–32.

13. **Weekly and biweekly magazines**

Note

5. Malcolm Gladwell, "Pandora's Briefcase," *New Yorker*, May 10, 2010, 72–78.

Bibliography

Gladwell, Malcolm. "Pandora's Briefcase." *New Yorker*, May 10, 2010, 72–78.

14. **Newspaper article**

Note

1. Melena Ryzik, "Off the Beaten Beat," *New York Times*, May 11, 2007, late edition, sec. E.

16d Online Sources in CMS Style

15. Document or page from a Web site

To cite original content from within a Web site, include as many descriptive elements as you can: author of the page, title of the page, title and owner of the Web site, and the URL. Include the date accessed only if the site is time-sensitive or is frequently updated. If you cannot locate an individual author, the owner of the site can stand in for the author.

Note

11. National Organization for Women, "NOW History," accessed October 8, 2013, http://www.now.org/history/history.html.

Bibliography

National Organization for Women. "NOW History." Accessed October 8, 2013. http://www.now.org.history/history.html.

16. Online book

Note

12. Angelina Grimké, *Appeal to the Christian Women of the South* (New York: New York Anti-Slavery Society, 1836), accessed November 2, 2010, http://history.furman.edu/~benson/docs/grimke2.htm.

Bibliography

Grimké, Angelina. *Appeal to the Christian Women of the South*. New York: New York Anti-Slavery Society, 1836. Accessed November 2, 2010. http://history.furman.edu/~benson/docs/grimke2.htm.

17. Online article

Note

13. Margaret Cohen, "Literary Studies on the Terraqueous Globe," *PMLA* 125, no. 3 (2010): 657–62, doi:10.1632/pmla.2010.125.3.657.

Bibliography

Cohen, Margaret. "Literary Studies on the Terraqueous Globe." *PMLA* 125, no. 3 (2010): 657–62. doi:10.1632/pmla.2010.125.3.657.

18. Posting to a discussion list or group

Note

16. Jason Marcel, post to US Politics Online Today in Politics Forum, April 4, 2004, http://www.uspoliticsonline.com/forums/forumdisplay.php?f=24.

19. E-mail

Because personal e-mails are not available to the public, they are not usually listed in the bibliography.

Note

11. Erik Lynn Williams, "Social Anxiety Disorder," e-mail to author, August 12, 2007.

16e Sample Pages with CMS Documentation

Laker 1

Jason Laker

American History 102

January 28, 2014

The Electoral College: Does It Have a Future?

Until the presidential election of 2000, few Americans thought much about the Electoral College. It was something they had learned about in civics class and had then forgotten about as other, more pressing bits of information required their attention. In November

2000, however, the Electoral College took center stage and sparked an argument that continues today: Should the Electoral College be abolished?

The founders of the new nation established the Electoral College as a compromise between elections by Congress and those by popular vote.[1] The Electoral College consists of a group of electors who meet to vote for the president and vice president of the United States. The electors are nominated by political parties within each state, and the number each state gets relates to the state's congressional delegation. The process and the ideas behind it sound simple, but the actual workings of the Electoral College remain a mystery to many Americans.

The complicated nature of the Electoral College is one of the reasons why some people want to see it abolished. One voter writes in a letter to the editor of the *New York Times* that the elimination of the Electoral College is necessary "to demystify our voting system in the eyes of foreigners and our own citizenry."[2] Other detractors claim that it just does not work, and they cite the presidential elections of 1824, 1876, 1888, and, of course, 2000 as representative of the failures of the Electoral College. Those who defend the Electoral College, however, claim that the failures of these elections have little to do with the Electoral College itself.[3]

According to Gary Gregg, director of the McConnell Center for Political Leadership, a new study shows that much of what Americans think we know about the Electoral College is wrong. Consequently, we should actively question the wisdom of those who want to see it abolished.[4]

Laker 6

NOTES

1. Lawrence D. Longley and Neal R. Peirce, *The Electoral College Primer 2000* (New Haven: Yale University Press, 1999).

2. William C. McIntyre, "Revisiting the Electoral College," *New York Times*, November 17, 2001, late edition, sec. A.

3. Avagara, *EC: The Electoral College Webzine*, accessed January 21, 2014, http://www.avagara.com/e_c/.

4. Gary Gregg, "Keep the College," *National Review Online*, November 7, 2001, accessed January 19, 2014, http://www.lexisnexis .com/universe/.

Laker 7

BIBLIOGRAPHY

Avagara. *EC: The Electoral College Webzine*. Accessed January 21, 2014. http://www.avagara.com/e_c/.

Gregg, Gary. "Keep the College." *National Review Online*. November 7, 2001. Accessed January 19, 2014. http://www.lexisnexis.com /universe/.

Longley, Lawrence D., and Neal R. Peirce. *The Electoral College Primer 2000*. New Haven: Yale University Press, 1999.

McIntyre, William C. "Revisiting the Electoral College." *New York Times*. November 17, 2001.

17 CSE Documentation

QUICK*TAKE*

- Cite books in CSE–style references (see pp. 151-152)
- Cite articles and online sources in CSE–style references (see pp. 153-154)

Widely followed by writers in the sciences is the comprehensive guide published by the Council of Science Editors (CSE): *Scientific Style and Format: The CSE Manual for Authors, Editors, and Publishers*, seventh edition (2006). The preferred documentation system in CSE places references in the body of the text, marked by a superscript number preceded by a space and placed inside punctuation.

> Cold fingers and toes are common circulatory problems found in most heavy cigarette smokers [1].

This number corresponds to a numbered entry on the CSE source list, titled *References*. To create a CSE References page, follow these guidelines.

1. Title your page *References* and center this title at the top of the page.
2. Single-space within citations and double-space between citations.
3. List citations in the order in which they appear in the body of the paper. Begin each citation with its citation number, followed by a period, flush left.
4. Authors are listed by last name, followed by initials. Capitalize only first words and proper nouns in cited titles. Book titles are not underlined, and article titles are not placed between quotation marks. Names of journals should be abbreviated where possible.
5. Cite publication year, and volume or page numbers if applicable.

17a In-text References in CSE Style

CSE documentation of sources does not require the names of authors in the text but only a number that refers to the References list at the end.

> In 1997, the Gallup poll reported that 55% of adults in the United States think secondhand smoke is "very harmful," compared to only 36% in 1994 [1].

The superscript [1] refers to the first entry on the References list, where readers will find a complete citation for this source.

What if you need more than one citation in a passage?

If the numbers are consecutive, separate them with a hyphen. If they are nonconsecutive, use only a comma.

> The previous work [1,3,5–8,11]

Index of CSE Documentation

Books and Nonperiodical Sources in CSE-style References

1. Nance JJ. What goes up: the global assault on our atmosphere. New York: W Morrow; 1991.

Author's or Editor's Name

The author's last name comes first, followed by the initials of the author's first name and middle name (if provided). If there is an editor, put the word *editor* after the name.

Book Title

- Do not italicize or underline titles.
- Capitalize only the first word and proper nouns.

Publication Information

Year of publication

- The year comes after the other publication information. It follows a semicolon.
- If it is a multivolume edited work published over a period of more than one year, give the span of years.

Page numbers

- When citing part of a book, give the page range for the selection: *p. 60–90*.

Sample references

1. Book by a single author/editor

2. Minger TJ, editor. Greenhouse glasnost: the crisis of global warming. New York (NY): Ecco; 1990.

2. Book by two or more authors/editors

3. O'Day DH, Horgen PA, editors. Sexual interactions in eukaryotic microbes. New York (NY): Academic Press; 1981.

3. Book by a group or organization

4. IAEA. Manual on radiation haematology. Vienna (Austria): IAEA; 1971.

4. Two or more books by the same author

Number the references according to the order in which they appear in the text.

5. Gould SJ. The structure of evolutionary theory. Cambridge (MA): Harvard University Press; 2002.

8. Gould SJ. Wonderful life: the Burgess Shale and the nature of history. New York (NY): Norton; 1989.

5. A selection in an anthology or a chapter in an edited collection

7. Kraft K, Baines DM. Computer classrooms and third grade development. In: Green MD, editor. Computers and early development. New York (NY): Academic; 1997. p. 168–179.

6. Technical and research reports

9. Austin A, Baldwin R, editors. Faculty collaboration: enhancing the quality of scholarship and teaching. ASCHE-ERIC Higher Education Report 7. Washington (DC): George Washington University; 1991.

Periodical Sources in CSE-style References

1. Bohannon J. Climate change: IPCC report lays out options for taming greenhouse gases. Science. 2007;316(5826): 812–814.

Author's Name

The author's last name comes first, followed by the initials of the author's first name and middle name (if provided).

Title of Article

- Do not place titles inside quotation marks.
- Capitalize only the first word and proper nouns.

Publication Information

Name of journal

- Do not abbreviate single-word journal titles. Abbreviate multiple-word journal titles according to the National Information Standards Organization (NISO) list of serials.
- Capitalize each word of the journal title, even if abbreviated.

Date of publication, volume, and issue numbers

- Include the issue number inside parentheses if it is present in the document. Leave no spaces between these items.

7. Article by one author

1. Board J. Reduced lodging for soybeans in low plant population is related to light quality. Crop Science. 2001;41:379–387.

8. Article by two or more authors/editors

2. Simms K, Denison D. Observed interactions between wild and domesticated mixed-breed canines. J Mamm. 1997;70:341–342.

9. Article by a group or organization

4. Center for Science in the Public Interest. Meat labeling: help! Nutrition Action Health Letter: 2. 2001 Apr 1.

10. Journals paginated by issue

Use the month or season of publication (and day, if given) for journals paginated by issue. Include the issue number in parentheses after the volume number.

8. Barlow JP. Africa rising: everything you know about Africa is wrong. Wired. 1998 Jan:142–158.

17d Online Sources in CSE-style References

11. Online journal articles

2. Schunck CH, Shin Y, Schirotzek A, Zwierlein MW, Ketterle A. Pairing without superfluidity: the ground state of an imbalanced fermi mixture. Science [Internet]. 2007 [cited 2007 Jun 15]; 316(5826):867–870. Available from: http://www.sciencemag.org/cgi/content/full/3165826/867/DC1

12. Scientific databases on the Internet

3. Comprehensive Large Array-data Stewardship System [Internet]. 2007. Release 4.2. Silver Spring (MD): National Environmental Satellite, Data, and Information Service (US). [updated 2007 May 2; cited 2007 May 14]. Available from: http://www.class.noaa.gov/saa/products/welcome

PART 4 Effective Style and Language

18 Write with Power

QUICK*TAKE*

- Make your writing active (see p. 157)
- Use agents in your writing (see p. 159)
- Vary your sentences (see p. 160)

In photographs

You imagine actions when subjects are captured in motion.

In writing

Your readers expect actions to be expressed in verbs:
gallop, canter, trot, run, sprint, dash, bound, thunder, tear away.

In photographs

Viewers interpret the most prominent person or thing as the subject—what the photograph is about.

In writing

Readers interpret the first person or thing they meet in a sentence as what the sentence is about (the jockey, the horse). They expect that person or thing to perform the action expressed in the verb.

18a Recognize Active and Passive Voice

In the **active voice**, the subject of the sentence is the actor. In the **passive voice**, the subject is being acted upon.

Active **Leonardo da Vinci** painted *Mona Lisa* between 1503 and 1506.

Passive ***Mona Lisa*** was painted by Leonardo da Vinci between 1503 and 1506.

To write with power, use the active voice. Observe the difference here.

Passive The pear tree in the front yard **was demolished** by the unexpected storm.

Active The unexpected storm **demolished** the pear tree in the front yard.

18b Use Action Verbs

Where are the action words in the following sentences?

> Red hair flying, professional snowboarder and skateboarder Shaun White became a two-time Olympic gold medalist with a record score of 48.4 at the 2010 Winter Olympics. White was a skier before he was five but became a snowboarder at age six, and by age seven, he had become a professional, receiving corporate sponsorships. At age nine, White became friends with professional skateboarder Tony Hawk, who became White's mentor in becoming a professional skateboarder. White is known for accomplishing several "firsts" in snowboarding, including being the first to land back-to-back double corks and to master a trick called a Cab 7 Melon Grab. He is also the holder of record for the highest score in the men's halfpipe at the Winter Olympics.

No action words here! The passage describes a series of actions, yet most of the verbs are *is*, *was*, and *became*. Think about what the actions are and choose powerful verbs that express those actions.

> Red hair flying, professional snowboarder and skateboarder Shaun White **scored** a 48.4 during the 2010 Winter Olympics and **won** his second gold medal. White **skied** before he was five but **switched** to snowboarding at age six, and by age seven **received** corporate sponsorships. At age nine, White **befriended** professional skateboarder Tony Hawk, who **mentored** White and **helped** him become a professional skateboarder. White **has accomplished** several "firsts" in snowboarding, including landing back-to-back double corks and mastering a trick called a Cab 7 Melon Grab. He also **holds** the record for the highest score in the men's halfpipe at the Winter Olympics.

Many sentences contain words that express action, but those words are nouns instead of verbs. Often the nouns can be changed into verbs. For example:

> The arson unit ~~conducted an investigation of~~ **investigated** the mysterious fire.
>
> The committee ~~had a debate over~~ **debated** how best to spend the surplus funds.

Notice that changing nouns into verbs also eliminates unnecessary words.

18c Find Agents

The **agent** is the person or thing that does the action. Powerful writing puts the agents in sentences.

Focus on people

Read the following sentence aloud.

> The use of a MIDI keyboard for playing the song will facilitate capturing it in digital form on a laptop for the subsequent purpose of uploading it to a Web site.

It sounds boring, doesn't it? Putting people into the sentence makes it come alive.

> By playing the song on a MIDI keyboard, **we** can record the digitized sound on **our** laptop and then upload it to **our** Web site.

Including people makes your writing more emphatic. Most readers relate better to people than to abstractions. Putting people in your sentences also introduces active verbs because people do things.

Identify characters

If people are not your subject, then keep the focus on other types of characters.

Without characters	The celebration of Martin Luther King Day had to be postponed because of inclement weather.
With characters	A severe **ice storm** forced the **city** to postpone the Martin Luther King Day celebration.

18d Vary Your Sentences

Read the following passage.

> On the first day Garth, Jim, and I paddled fourteen miles down Johnstone Strait. The next day we headed down the strait about five more miles to Robson Bight. It is a famous scratching place for orcas. The Bight is a small bay. We paddled out into the strait so we could see the entire Bight. There were no orcas inside. By this time we were getting tired. We were hungry. The clouds assumed a wintry dark thickness. The wind was kicking up against us. Our heads were down going into the cold spray.

The subject matter is interesting, but the writing isn't. The passage is a series of short sentences, one after the other. When you have too many short sentences one after the other, try combining a few of them.

The result of combining some (but not all) short sentences is a paragraph whose sentences match the interest of the subject.

> On the first day Garth, Jim, and I paddled fourteen miles down Johnstone Strait. The next day we headed down the strait about five more miles to Robson Bight, a small bay known as a famous scratching place for orcas. We paddled out into the strait so we could see the entire Bight, but there were no orcas inside. By this time we were tired and hungry, the clouds had assumed a wintry dark thickness, and the wind was kicking up against us—our heads dropped going into the cold spray.

19 Write Concisely

QUICK*TAKE*

- Eliminate unnecessary words (see below)
- Reduce wordy phrases (see below)
- Simplify tangled sentences (see p. 163)

19a Eliminate Unnecessary Words

Clutter creeps into our lives every day. Clutter also creeps into writing through unnecessary words, inflated constructions, and excessive jargon.

> In regards to the Web site, the content is pretty successful in consideration of the topic. The site is fairly good writing-wise and is very unique in telling you how to adjust the rear derailleur one step at a time.

The words in orange are clutter. Get rid of the clutter. You can say the same thing with half the words and gain more impact as a result.

> The well-written Web site on bicycle repair provides step-by-step instructions on adjusting your rear derailleur.

Redundancy

Some words act as modifiers, but when you look closely at them, they repeat the meaning of the word they pretend to modify. Have you heard a store advertise "Come in for a *free gift*?" Aren't gifts free by definition? Likewise, you may have heard expressions such as *red in color, small in size, round in shape,* or *honest truth.* Imagine *red* not referring to color or *round* not referring to shape.

19b Reduce Wordy Phrases

Many inexperienced writers use phrases like "It is my opinion that" or "I think that" to begin sentences. These phrases are deadly to read. If you find them in your prose, cut them. Unless a writer is citing a source, we assume that the ideas are the writer's.

Coaches are among the worst at using many words for what could be said in a few.

> After much deliberation about Brown's future in football with regard to possible permanent injuries, I came to the conclusion that it would be in his best interest not to continue his pursuit of playing football again.

The coach might have said simply

> Because Brown risks permanent injury if he plays football again, I decided to release him from the team.

Perhaps the coach wanted to sound impressive, authoritative, or thoughtful. But the result is the opposite. Speakers and writers who impress us are those who use words efficiently.

COMMON ERRORS

Edit Help

Empty intensifiers

Intensifiers modify verbs, adjectives, and other adverbs, and they are often overused. One of the most overused intensifiers is *very*.

Empty intensifier Her clothing style was **very unique**.

If something is unique, it is one of a kind. The word *very* doesn't make something more than unique.

Improved Her clothing style was **unique**.

Or

Improved Her clothing style was **strange**.

Very and *totally* are but two of a list of empty intensifiers that can usually be eliminated with no loss of meaning. Other empty intensifiers include *absolutely, awfully, definitely, incredibly, particularly,* and *really.*

Remember: When you use *very, totally,* or another intensifier before an adjective or adverb, ask yourself whether a more accurate adjective or adverb could express the same thought.

WORDY PHRASES

Certain stock phrases plague writing in the workplace, in the media, and in academia. Many can be replaced by one or two words with no loss in meaning.

Wordy	Concise
at this point in time	now
due to the fact that	because
for the purpose of	for
have the ability to	can
in spite of the fact that	although
in the event that	if

19c Simplify Tangled Sentences

Long sentences can be graceful and forceful. Such sentences, however, often require several revisions before they achieve elegance. Too often long sentences reflect wandering thoughts that the writer did not bother to go back and sort out. Two of the most important strategies for untangling long sentences are described in Chapter 18: using active verbs (Section 18b) and finding your agents (Section 18c). Here are some other strategies.

Revise expletives

Expletives are empty words that can occupy the subject position in a sentence. The most frequently used expletives are *there is, there are,* and *it is.*

Wordy There were several important differences between the positions raised by the candidates in the debate.

To simplify the sentence, find the agent and make it the subject.

Revised The two candidates raised several important differences between their positions in the debate.

A few kinds of sentences—for example, *It is raining*—do require you to use an expletive. In most cases, however, expletives add unnecessary words, and sentences will read better without them.

Use positive constructions

Sentences become wordy and hard to read when they include two or more negatives, such as the words *no, not,* and *nor,* plus the prefix *un-* or *mis-*. For example:

Difficult	A **not un**common complaint among employers of new college graduates is that they cannot communicate effectively in writing.
Revised	Employers frequently complain that new college graduates cannot write effectively.
Even simpler	Employers value the rare college graduate who can write well.

Phrasing sentences positively usually makes them more economical. Moreover, it makes your style more forceful and direct.

Simplify sentence structure

Long sentences can be hard to read, not because they are long but because they are convoluted and hide the relationships among ideas. Take the following sentence as an example.

> Some historians are arguing that World War II actually ended with German reunification in 1990 instead of when the Japanese surrendered in 1945, after which time the Cold War got in the way of formal legal settlements among the involved nations and Germany was divided between the Western powers and the Soviet Union meaning that no comprehensive peace treaty was signed.

This sentence is hard to read. To rewrite sentences like this one, find the main ideas and then determine the relationships among them.

After examining the sentence, you decide there are two key ideas:

1. Some historians argue that World War II actually ended in 1990 with German reunification, not when the Japanese surrendered in 1945.

> 2 The Cold War and the division of Germany between the Western powers and the Soviet Union hindered formal legal settlements among the involved nations.

Next, ask what the relationship is between the two ideas. When you identify the key ideas, the relationship is often obvious; in this case, (2) is the cause of (1). Thus, the word you want to connect the two ideas is *because*.

> **Because** the Cold War and the division of Germany between the Western powers and the Soviet Union hindered formal legal settlements among the involved nations, some historians argue that World War II actually ended in 1990 with German reunification rather than with the Japanese surrender in 1945.

The revised sentence is both clearer and more concise, reducing the number of words from sixty-one to forty-seven.

20 Write with Emphasis

QUICK*TAKE*

- Manage emphasis in your sentences (see p. 166)
- Use parallelism correctly (see p. 169)

Photographs and writing gain energy when key ideas are emphasized.

In visuals

Photographers create emphasis by composing the image to direct the attention of the viewer. Putting people and objects in the foreground and making them stand out against the background gives them emphasis.

In writing

Writers have many tools for creating emphasis. Writers can design a page to gain emphasis by using headings, white space, type size, color, and boldfacing. Just as important, learning the craft of structuring sentences will empower you to give your writing emphasis.

20a Manage Emphasis Within Sentences

Put your main ideas in main clauses

Placing more important information in **main clauses** and less important information in subordinate clauses emphasizes what is important.

In the following paragraph, all the sentences are main clauses.

> Lotteries were common in the United States before and after the American Revolution. They eventually ran into trouble. They were run by private companies. Sometimes the companies took off with the money. They didn't pay the winners.

This paragraph is grammatically correct, but it does not help the reader understand which pieces of information the author wants to emphasize. Combining the simple sentences into main and subordinate clauses and phrases can significantly improve the paragraph.

First, identify the main ideas.

Lotteries were common in the United States before and after the American Revolution. They eventually ran into trouble.

These ideas can be combined into one sentence.

Lotteries were common in the United States before and after the American Revolution, but they eventually ran into trouble.

Now think about the relationship of the three remaining sentences to the main ideas. Those sentences explain why lotteries ran into trouble; thus, the relationship is *because*.

> Lotteries were common in the United States before and after the American Revolution, but they eventually ran into trouble **because** they were run by private companies that sometimes took off with the money instead of paying the winners.

Put key ideas at the beginning and end of sentences

Read these sentences aloud.

1. The **Cottingley Fairies**, a series of five photographs taken in 1917 by Elsie Wright and Frances Griffiths, depicts the girls interacting with what seem to be fairies.
2. A series of photographs showing two girls interacting with what seem to be fairies, known as the **Cottingley Fairies**, was taken by Elsie Wright and Frances Griffiths in 1917.
3. The series of photos Elsie Wright and Frances Griffiths took in 1917 showing two girls interacting with what seem to be fairies is called the **Cottingley Fairies**.

Most readers put the primary emphasis on words at the beginning and end of a sentence. The front of a sentence usually gives what is known: the topic. At the back is the new information about the topic. Subordinate information is in the middle. If a paragraph is about the Cottingley Fairies, we would not expect the writer to choose sentence 2 over 1 or 3. In sentence 2, the reference to the Cottingley Fairies is buried in the middle.

 Forge Links Across Sentences

When your writing maintains a focus of attention across sentences, the reader can distinguish the important ideas and how they relate to each other. To achieve this coherence, you need to control which ideas occupy the positions of greatest emphasis. The words you repeat from sentence to sentence act as links.

Link sentences from front to front

In front-to-front linkage, the subject of the sentence remains the focus from one sentence to the next. In the following sequence, sentences 1 through 5 are all about Arthur Wright. The subject of each sentence refers to the first sentence with the pronouns *he* and *his*.

1 **Arthur Wright** was one of the first electrical engineers in England.

2 **He** loaned his camera to his daughter Elsie, who took the fairy pictures in the yard behind their house.

3 **His** opinion was that the pictures were fake.

4 However, **his** wife, Polly, was convinced that they were real.

5 Nevertheless, **he** banned Elsie from ever using his camera again.

Each sentence adds more information about the repeated topic, Arthur Wright.

Link sentences from back to front

In back-to-front linkage, the new information at the end of the sentence is used as the topic of the next sentence. Back-to-front linkage allows new material to be introduced and commented on.

1 By the summer of 1919, the girls and their photographs had become so well known that author Sir Arthur Conan Doyle even wrote an article for a leading magazine claiming that the photos and the fairies were **real**.

2 Not everyone believed that the Cottingley Fairies were **authentic**, however, and other public figures wrote the papers calling the photographs a **hoax**.

3 The **hoax** continued until the 1980s, when both Elsie and Frances finally admitted that all but one of the pictures were fake.

Back-to-front linkage is useful when ideas need to be advanced quickly, as when you are telling stories. Rarely, however, will you use either front-to-front linkage or back-to-front linkage continuously throughout a piece of writing. Use front-to-front linkage to add more information and back-to-front linkage to move the topic along.

Check the links between your sentences to find any gaps that will cause your readers to stumble.

20c Use Parallel Structure with Parallel Ideas

What if Patrick Henry had written "Give me liberty or I prefer not to live"? Would we remember those words today? We remember the words he did use: "Give me liberty or give me death." Writers who use parallel structure often create memorable sentences.

Use parallelism with *and, or, nor, but*

When you join elements with coordinating conjunctions (*and, or, nor, yet, so, but,* and *for*), normally you should use parallel grammatical structure for those elements.

Awkward

In today's global economy, the method of production and where factories are located has become relatively unimportant in comparison with the creation of new concepts and marketing those concepts.

Parallel

In today's global economy, how goods are made and where they are produced has become relatively unimportant in comparison with creating new concepts and marketing those concepts.

Use parallelism with *either/or, not only/but also*

Make identical in structure the parts of sentences linked by correlative conjunctions: *either . . . or, neither . . . nor, not only . . . but also, whether . . . or.*

Awkward

Purchasing the undeveloped land **not only** gives us a new park **but also** it is something that our children will benefit from in the future.

Parallel

Purchasing the undeveloped land **not only** will give our city a new park **but also** will leave our children a lasting inheritance.

The more structural elements you match, the stronger the effect that parallelism will achieve.

COMMON ERRORS

Faulty parallel structure

When writers neglect to use parallel structure, the result can be jarring. Reading your writing aloud will help you catch problems in parallelism. Read this sentence aloud.

Not parallel At our club meeting, we identified problems in finding new members, publicizing our activities, and maintenance of our Web site.

The end of the sentence does not sound right because the parallel structure is broken. We expect to find another verb + *ing* following *finding* and *publicizing*. Instead, we run into *maintenance,* a noun. The problem is easy to fix: Change the noun to the *-ing* verb form.

Parallel At our club meeting, we identified problems in finding new members, publicizing our activities, and maintaining our Web site.

Remember: Use parallel structure for parallel ideas.

21 Find the Right Words

QUICK*TAKE*

- Choose the right level of formality (see below)
- Write to be inclusive (see p. 173)

21a Be Aware of Levels of Formality

While you may get plenty of practice in informal writing—e-mails and notes to friends and family members—mastering formal writing is essential in academic and professional settings. How formal or informal should your writing be? That depends on your audience and the writing task at hand.

Colloquialisms

Colloquialisms are words or expressions that are used informally, often in conversation but less often in writing.

> I'm not happy with my grades, but that's the way **the cookie crumbles**.
>
> Liz is always **running off at the mouth** about something.
>
> I enjoyed the restaurant, but it was **nothing to write home about**.

In academic and professional writing, colloquialisms often suggest a flippant attitude, carelessness, or even thoughtlessness. Sometimes colloquialisms can be used for ironic or humorous effect, but as a general rule, if you want to be taken seriously, avoid using them.

Avoiding colloquialisms does not mean, however, that you should use big words when small ones will just do as well or that you should use ten words instead of two. Formality does not mean being pretentious or wordy.

Wordy

> In this writer's opinion, one could argue that the beaches on the west coast of Florida are far superior to their counterparts on the east coast.

Better

Florida's west coast beaches are better than those on the east coast.

Slang

The most conspicuous kind of language that is usually avoided in formal writing is slang. The next time a friend talks to you, listen closely to the words he or she uses. Chances are you will notice several words that you probably would not use in a college writing assignment. Slang words are created by and for a particular group—even if that group is just you and your friend.

> The party was **bumpin** with all my **peeps**.
>
> Joey's new **ride** is totally **pimped** out.

Slang is used to indicate membership in a particular group. But because slang excludes readers who are not members of the group, it is best avoided in academic writing.

21b Be Aware of Denotation and Connotation

Words have both literal meanings, called **denotations**, and associated meanings, called **connotations**. The contrast is evident in words that mean roughly the same thing but have different connotations. For example, some people are set in their opinions, a quality that can be described positively as *persistent, firm,* and *steadfast* or negatively as *stubborn, bull-headed,* and *close-minded.*

Use Specific Language

Be precise

Effective writing conveys information clearly and precisely. Words such as *situation, sort, thing, aspect,* and *kind* often signal undeveloped or even lazy thinking.

Vague The violence aspect determines how video games are rated.

Better The level of violence determines how video games are rated.

When citing numbers or quantities, be as exact as possible. A precise number, if known, is always better than slippery words like *several* or *many,* which some writers use to cloak the fact that they don't know the quantity in question.

Use a dictionary

There is no greater tool for writers than the dictionary. Always have a dictionary handy when you write—either a book or an online version—and get into the habit of using it. In addition to checking spelling, you can find additional meanings of a word that perhaps you had not considered, and you can find the etymology—the origins of a word. In many cases, knowing the etymology of a word can help you use it to better effect. For example, if you want to argue that universities as institutions have succeeded because they bring people together in contexts that prepare them for their lives after college, you might point out the etymology of *university. University* can be traced back to the late Latin word *universitas,* which means "society or guild," thus emphasizing the idea of a community of learning.

21d Write to Be Inclusive

While the conventions of language change continually, three guidelines for inclusive language toward all groups remain constant.

- Do not point out people's differences unless those differences are relevant to your argument.
- Call people whatever they prefer to be called.
- When given a choice of terms, choose the more accurate one. (*Vietnamese*, for example, is preferable to *Asian*.)

Be inclusive about gender

Don't use masculine nouns and pronouns to refer to both men and women. *He, his, him, man,* and *mankind* are outmoded and inaccurate terms for both genders. Eliminate gender bias by using the following tips.

- Don't say *boy* when you can say *child.*
- Use *men and women* or *people* instead of *man.*
- Use *humanity* or *humankind* in place of *mankind.*

Eliminating *he, his,* and *him* when referring to both men and women is more complicated. Many readers consider *he/she* to be an awkward alternative. Try one of the following strategies instead.

- Make the noun and its corresponding pronoun plural. The pronoun will change from *he, him,* or *his* to *they, them,* or *theirs.*

Biased Masculine Pronouns

An undercover agent won't reveal **his** identity, even to other agents, if **he** thinks doing so will jeopardize the case.

Better

Undercover agents won't reveal **their** identities, even to other agents, if **they** think doing so will jeopardize the case.

- Replace the pronoun with an article (*the*, *a*, or *an*)

Biased Masculine Pronoun

Each prospective driving instructor must pass a state test before receiving **his** license.

Better

Each prospective driving instructor must pass a state test before receiving **a** license.

Be inclusive about race and ethnicity

Use the terms for racial and ethnic groups that the groups use for themselves. Use *black* to write about members of the Black Coaches' Association and *African American* to write about members of the Society for African American Brotherhood.

When discussing an American's heritage, often the best term to use is the country of origin plus the word *American,* as in *Swedish American* or *Mexican American* (note that these terms are not hyphenated). Currently, *black* and *African American* are acceptable.

Some people prefer *Native American* over *American Indian*, but both terms are used. In Canada the preferred name for indigenous peoples is either *First Nations* or *First Peoples* (or *Inuit* for those who live in the far north). *First Peoples* and *First Nations* are increasingly used by indigenous peoples in the United States in solidarity with their Canadian relatives. If you are writing about specific people, use the name of the specific American or Canadian Indian group (*Cree, Hopi, Mi'kmaq, Ute*).

Be inclusive about people with disabilities

The *Publication Manual of the American Psychological Association* (6th ed.) offers some good advice about putting people first, not their disabilities (76). Write *people who are deaf* instead of *the deaf* and *a student who is quadriplegic* instead of *a quadriplegic student.* Don't reduce people to their deficiencies.

Be inclusive about people of different ages

Avoid bias by choosing accurate terms to describe age. If possible, use the person's age. *Eighty-two-year-old Adele Schumacher* is better than *elderly Adele Schumacher.*

 Recognize International Varieties of English

English today comes in various shapes and forms. Many applied linguists now speak of "World Englishes" in the plural, to highlight the diversity of the English language as it is used worldwide.

English has long been established as the dominant language in Australia, Canada, New Zealand, the United Kingdom, and the United States, although many people in those countries also use other languages at home and in their communities. Englishes used in these countries share many characteristics, but there also are some differences in sentence structure, vocabulary, spelling, and punctuation. For example:

British English	The outdoor concert was **rained off**.
U.S. English	The outdoor concert was **rained out**.
British English	What's the price of **petrol** (petroleum) these days?
U.S. English	What's the price of **gas** (gasoline) these days?

Newer varieties of English have emerged outside traditionally English-speaking countries. Many former British and U.S. colonies—Hong Kong, India, Malaysia, Nigeria, Papua New Guinea, the Philippines, Singapore, and others—continue to use a local variety of English for both public and private communication. Englishes used in many of these countries are based primarily on the British variety, but they also include many features that reflect the local context.

Indian English	**Open** the air conditioner.
U.S. English	**Turn on** the air conditioner.
Singaporean English	I was **arrowed** to lead the discussion.
U.S. English	I was **selected** to lead the discussion.

Remember that correctness differs from one variation of English to another.

PART 5

Understanding Grammar

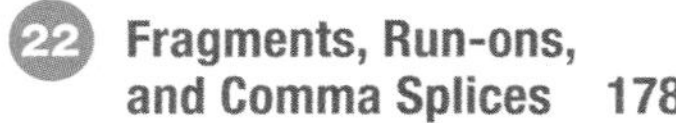

22 Fragments, Run-ons, and Comma Splices

QUICK*TAKE*

- Identify and correct fragments (see below)
- Identify and correct run-on sentences (see p. 180)
- Identify and correct comma splices (see p. 182)

Fragments

Fragments are incomplete sentences. They are punctuated to look like sentences, but they lack a key element—often a subject or a verb—or else they are subordinate clauses or phrases. Consider this example of a full sentence followed by a fragment.

> The university's enrollment rose unexpectedly during the fall semester. **Because the percentage of students who accepted offers of admission was much higher than in previous years and fewer students than usual dropped out or transferred.**

When a sentence starts with *because,* we expect to find a main clause later. Instead, the *because* clause refers back to the previous sentence. The writer no doubt knew that the fragment gave the reasons why enrollment rose, but a reader must stop to determine the connection.

In formal writing, you should avoid fragments. Readers expect words punctuated as a sentence to be a complete sentence. They expect writers to complete their thoughts rather than force readers to guess the missing element.

Basic strategies for turning fragments into sentences

Incorporate the fragment into an adjoining sentence. In many cases, you can incorporate the fragment into an adjoining sentence.

> I was hooked on the ~~game. Playing~~ game, playing day and night.

Add the missing element. If you cannot incorporate a fragment into another sentence, add the missing element.

> When aiming for the highest returns, ~~and~~ *investors* also ~~thinking~~ *should think* about the possible losses.

COMMON ERRORS

Recognizing fragments

If you can spot fragments, you can fix them. Grammar checkers can find some of them, but they miss many fragments and may identify other sentences wrongly as fragments. Ask these questions when you are checking for sentence fragments.

- **Does the sentence have a subject?** Except for commands, sentences need subjects.

  Incorrect Jane spent every cent of credit she had available. And then applied for more cards.

- **Does the sentence have a complete verb?** Sentences require complete verbs. Verbs that end in *-ing* must have an auxiliary verb to be complete.

  Incorrect Ralph keeps changing majors. He trying to figure out what he really wants to do after college.

- **If the sentence begins with a subordinate clause, is there a main clause in the same sentence?**

  Incorrect Even though Seattle is cloudy much of the year, no American city is more beautiful when the sun shines. Which is one reason people continue to move there.

Remember:

1. **A sentence must have a subject and a complete verb.**
2. **A subordinate clause cannot stand alone as a sentence.**

22b Run-on Sentences

While fragments are incomplete sentences, run-ons (also called "fused sentences") jam together two or more sentences, failing to separate them with appropriate punctuation.

Fixing run-on sentences

Take three steps to fix run-on sentences: (1) identify the problem, (2) determine where the run-on sentence needs to be divided, and (3) choose the punctuation that best indicates the relationship between the main clauses.

COMMON ERRORS

Recognizing run-on sentences

When you read this sentence, you realize something is wrong.

Incorrect I do not recall what kind of printer it was all I remember is that it could sort, staple, and print a packet at the same time.

The problem is that two main clauses are not separated by punctuation. The reader must look carefully to determine where one main clause stops and the next one begins.

> I do not recall what kind of printer it was | all I remember is that it could sort, staple, and print a packet at the same time.

A period should be placed after *was,* and the next sentence should begin with a capital letter.

Correct I do not recall what kind of printer it was. All I remember is that it could sort, staple, and print a packet at the same time.

Run-on sentences are major errors.

Remember: Two main clauses must be separated by correct punctuation.

1. Identify the problem. When you read your writing aloud, run-on sentences will often trip you up, just as they confuse readers. If you find two main clauses with no punctuation separating them, you have a run-on sentence. You can also search for subject and verb pairs to check for run-ons.

> SUBJ / VERB
> **Internet businesses are** not **bound** to specific locations or old ways of running a business **they are** more flexible in allowing employees to telecommute and to determine the hours they work.
> (S: they; V: are)

2. Determine where the run-on sentence needs to be divided.

> Internet businesses are not bound to specific locations or old ways of running a business | they are more flexible in allowing employees to telecommute and to determine the hours they work.

3. Determine the relationship between the main clauses. You will revise a run-on more effectively if you first determine the relationship between the main clauses and understand the effect or point you are trying to make. There are several punctuation strategies for fixing run-ons.

- **Insert a period.** This is the simplest way to fix a run-on sentence.

  Internet businesses are not bound to specific locations or old ways of running a business. They are more flexible in allowing employees to telecommute and to determine the hours they work.

  However, if you want to indicate more clearly a closer relationship between the two main clauses, you may want to choose one of the following strategies.

- **Insert a semicolon (and possibly a transitional word specifying the relationship between the two main clauses).**

  Internet businesses are not bound to specific locations or old ways of running a business; **therefore,** they are more flexible in allowing employees to telecommute and to determine the hours they work.

- **Insert a comma and a coordinating conjunction (*and, but, or, nor, for, so, yet*).**

  Internet businesses are not bound to specific locations or old ways of running a business, **so** they are more flexible in allowing employees to telecommute and to determine the hours they work.

- **Make one of the clauses subordinate.**

  Because Internet businesses are not bound to specific locations or old ways of running a business, they are more flexible in allowing employees to telecommute and to determine the hours they work.

22c Comma Splices

Comma splices occur when two or more sentences are incorrectly joined by a comma. A comma should not be used to link two clauses that could stand on their own. In this example, the comma following "classes" should be a period.

> **Most of us were taking the same classes, if someone had a question, we would all help out.**

Such sentences include a punctuation mark—a comma—separating two main clauses. However, a comma is not a strong enough punctuation mark to separate two main clauses.

COMMON ERRORS

Recognizing comma splices

When you edit your writing, look carefully at sentences that contain commas. Does the sentence contain two main clauses? If so, are the main clauses joined by a comma and a coordinating conjunction (*and, but, for, or, not, so, yet*)?

Incorrect The concept [SUBJ] of "nature" depends [VERB] on the concept of human "culture," the problem [SUBJ] is [V] that "culture" is itself shaped by "nature." [Two main clauses joined by only a comma]

Correct Even though the concept of "nature" depends on the concept of human "culture," "culture" is itself shaped by "nature." [Subordinate clause plus a main clause]

Correct The concept of "nature" depends on the concept of human "culture," but "culture" is itself shaped by "nature." [Two main clauses joined by a comma and a coordinating conjunction]

COMMON ERRORS

The word *however* produces some of the most common comma splice errors. When *however* begins a main clause, it should be preceded by a semicolon or a period, not a comma.

Incorrect The White House press secretary repeatedly vowed the administration was not choosing a side between the two countries embroiled in conflict, however the developing foreign policy suggested otherwise.

Correct The White House press secretary repeatedly vowed the administration was not choosing a side between the two countries embroiled in conflict; however, the developing foreign policy suggested otherwise. [Two main clauses joined by a semicolon]

Remember: Do not use a comma as a period.

Fixing comma splices

You have several options for fixing comma splices. Select the one that best fits where the sentence is located and the effect you are trying to achieve.

1. Change the comma to a period. Most comma splices can be fixed by changing the comma to a period.

It didn't matter that I worked in a windowless room for forty hours a ~~week, on~~ week. On the Web I was exploring and learning more about distant people and places than I ever had before.

2. Change the comma to a semicolon. A semicolon indicates a close connection between two main clauses.

It didn't matter that I worked in a windowless room for forty hours a ~~week,~~ week; on the Web I was exploring and learning more about distant people and places than I ever had before.

3. Insert a coordinating conjunction. Other comma splices can be repaired by inserting a coordinating conjunction (*and, but, or, nor, so, yet, for*) to indicate the relationship of the two main clauses. The coordinating conjunction must be preceded by a comma.

> Digital technologies have intensified a global culture that affects us daily in large and small ways, **yet** their impact remains poorly understood.

4. Make one of the main clauses a subordinate clause. If a comma splice includes one main clause that is subordinate to the other, rewrite the sentence using a subordinating conjunction (such as *after, although, because, if*).

> Because community
> ~~Community~~ is the vision of a great society trimmed down to the size of a small town, it is a powerful metaphor for real estate developers who sell a mini-utopia along with a house or condo.

5. Make one of the main clauses a phrase. You can also rewrite one of the main clauses as a phrase.

> Community—**the vision of a great society trimmed down to the size of a small town**—is a powerful metaphor for real estate developers who sell a mini-utopia along with a house or condo.

23 Subject-Verb Agreement

QUICK*TAKE*

- Decide whether a subject is singular or plural (see p. 185)
- Choose the right verb for indefinite pronouns (see p. 187)

23a Agreement in the Present Tense

When your verb is in the present tense, agreement in number is straightforward: The subject takes the base form of the verb in all but the third person singular. For example, the verb *walk,* in the present tense, agrees in number with most subjects in its base form.

First person singular	I walk
Second person singular	You walk
First person plural	We walk
Second person plural	You walk
Third person plural	They walk

Third person singular subjects are the exception to this rule. When your subject is in the third person singular (*he, it, Fido, Lucy, Mr. Jones*), you need to add *s* or *es* to the base form of the verb.

Third person singular (add *s*)	He walks. It walks. Fido walks.
Third person singular (add *es*)	Lucy goes. Mr. Jones goes.

23b Singular and Plural Subjects

Follow these rules when you have trouble determining whether to use a singular or plural verb form.

Subjects joined by *and*

When two subjects are joined by *and,* treat them as a compound (plural) subject.

> **Mary and Jane** are leaving for New York in the morning.

Some compound subjects work together as a single noun and are treated as singular. Although they appear to be compound and therefore plural, these subjects take the singular form of the verb.

> **Rock and roll** remains the devil's music, even in the twenty-first century.

When two nouns linked by *and* are modified by *every* or *each,* these two nouns are likewise treated as one singular subject.

> **Each night and day** brings no new news of you.

Subjects joined by *or*, *either . . . or*, or *neither . . . nor*

When a subject is joined by *or, either . . . or,* or *neither . . . nor,* make sure the verb agrees with the subject closest to the verb.

> SING — PLURAL — PL
> Is it **the sky or the mountains** that are blue?
>
> PLURAL — SING — SING
> Is it **the mountains or the sky** that **surrounds** us?
>
> PLURAL — SING — SING
> **Neither the animals nor the zookeeper** knows how to relock the gate.
>
> SING — PLURAL — PL
> **Either a coyote or several dogs** were howling last night.

Subjects along with another noun

Verbs agree with the subject of a sentence, even when a subject is linked to another noun with a phrase like *as well as, along with,* or *alongside.* These modifying phrases are usually set off from the main subject with commas.

> IGNORE THIS PHRASE
> **Chicken**, alongside various steamed vegetables, is my favorite meal.
>
> IGNORE THIS PHRASE
> Besides B. B. King, **John Lee Hooker and Muddy Waters** are my favorite blues artists of all time.

COMMON ERRORS

Subjects separated from verbs

The most common agreement errors occur when words come between the subject and verb. These intervening words do not affect subject-verb agreement. To ensure that you use the correct verb form, identify the subject and the verb. Ignore any phrases that come between them.

Incorrect (IGNORE THIS PHRASE: at inner-city Washington High) **Students** at inner-city Washington High **reads** more than suburban students.

Correct **Students** at inner-city Washington High **read** more than suburban students.

Students is plural and *read* is plural; subject and verb agree.

Incorrect **The whale shark**, the largest of all sharks, **feed** on plankton.

Correct **The whale shark,** the largest of all sharks, **feeds** on plankton.

COMMON ERRORS

The plural noun *sharks* that appears between the subject *the whale shark* and the verb *feeds* does not change the number of the subject. The subject is singular and the verb is singular. Subject and verb agree.

Remember: When you check for subject-verb agreement, identify the subject and the verb. Ignore any words that come between them.

23c Indefinite Pronouns as Subjects

The choice of a singular or plural pronoun is determined by the **antecedent**—the noun that pronoun refers to. Indefinite pronouns, such as *some, few, all, someone, everyone,* and *each,* often do not refer to identifiable subjects; hence, they have no antecedents. Most indefinite pronouns are singular and agree with the singular forms of verbs. Some, like *both* and *many,* are always plural and agree with the plural forms of verbs. Other indefinite pronouns are variable and can agree with either singular or plural verb forms, depending on the context of the sentence.

COMMON ERRORS

Agreement errors using *each*

When a pronoun is singular, its verb must be singular. A common stumbling block to this rule is the pronoun *each. Each* is always treated as a singular pronoun in college writing. When *each* stands alone, the choice is easy to make.

Incorrect Each are an outstanding student.

Correct Each is an outstanding student.

But when *each* is modified by a phrase that includes a plural noun, the choice of a singular verb form becomes less obvious.

Incorrect **Each** of the girls are fit.

Correct **Each** of the girls is fit.

Incorrect **Each** of our dogs get a present.

Correct **Each** of our dogs gets a present.

Remember: *Each* is always singular.

 Collective Nouns as Subjects

Collective nouns refer to groups (*audience, class, committee, crowd, family, government, group, jury, public, team*). When members of a group are considered as a unit, use singular verbs and singular pronouns.

> The **crowd** is unusually quiet at the moment, but it will get noisy soon.

When members of a group are considered as individuals, use plural verbs and plural pronouns.

> The **faculty** have their differing opinions on how to address the problems caused by reduced state support.

 Amounts, Numbers, and Pairs

Subjects that describe amounts of money, time, distance, or measurement are singular and require singular verbs.

> **Three days** is never long enough to unwind.

Some subjects, such as courses of study, academic specializations, illnesses, and even some nations, are treated as singular subjects even though their names end in *-s* or *-es*. For example, *economics, news, ethics, measles,* and *the United States* all end in *-s* but are all singular subjects.

> **Economics** is a rich field of study.

Other subjects require a plural verb form even though they refer to single items such as *jeans, slacks, glasses, scissors,* and *tweezers*. These items are all treated as pairs.

> My **glasses** are scratched.

24 Verbs

QUICK*TAKE*

- Understand basic verb forms (see below)
- Distinguish forms of transitive and intransitive verbs (see p. 192)

24a Basic Verb Forms

Almost all verbs in English have five possible forms. The exception is the verb *be*. Regular verbs follow this basic pattern.

Base form	Third-person singular	Past tense	Past participle	Present participle
jump	jumps	jumped	jumped	jumping
like	likes	liked	liked	liking
talk	talks	talked	talked	talking
wish	wishes	wished	wished	wishing

Base form

The base form of the verb is the one you find listed in the dictionary. This form indicates an action or condition in the present.

I **like** New York in June.

Third person singular

Third person singular subjects include *he, she, it,* and the nouns they replace, as well as other pronouns, including *someone, anybody,* and *everything.* Present tense verbs in the third person singular end with *-s* or *-es.*

Ms. Nessan **speaks** in riddles.

Past tense

The past tense describes an action or condition that occurred in the past. For most verbs, the past tense is formed by adding *-d* or *-ed* to the base form of the verb.

> She **inhaled** the night air.

Many verbs, however, have irregular past tense forms. (See Section 24b.)

Past participle

The past participle is used with *have* to form verbs in the perfect tense, with *be* to form verbs in the passive voice (see Section 18a), and to form adjectives derived from verbs.

Past perfect	They **had gone** to the grocery store prematurely.
Passive	The book **was written** thirty years before it **was published**.
Adjective	In the eighties, **teased** hair was all the rage.

COMMON ERRORS

Missing verb endings

Verb endings are not always pronounced in speech, especially in some dialects of English. It's also easy to omit these endings when you are writing quickly. Spelling checkers will not mark these errors, so you have to find them while proofreading.

Incorrect	Jeremy **feel** as if he's catching a cold.
Correct	Jeremy **feels** as if he's catching a cold.
Incorrect	Sheila **hope** she would get the day off.
Correct	Sheila **hoped** she would get the day off.

Remember: Check verbs carefully for missing *-s* or *-es* endings in the present tense and missing *d* or *ed* endings in the past tense.

Present participle

The present participle functions in one of three ways. Used with an auxiliary verb, it can describe a continuing action. The present participle can also function as a noun, known as a **gerund**, or as an adjective. The present participle is formed by adding *-ing* to the base form of a verb.

Present participle	Wild elks **are** competing for limited food resources.
Gerund	Sailing around the Cape of Good Hope is rumored to bring good luck.
Adjective	We looked for shells in the ebbing tide.

24b Irregular Verbs

A verb is **regular** when its past and past participle forms are created by adding *-ed* or *-d* to the base form. If this rule does not apply, the verb is considered an **irregular** verb. Here are selected common irregular verbs and their basic forms.

Common irregular verbs

Base form	Past tense	Past participle
be (is, am, are)	was, were	been
become	became	become
bring	brought	brought
come	came	come
do	did	done
get	got	got or gotten
have	had	had
go	went	gone
know	knew	known
see	saw	seen

COMMON ERRORS

Past tense forms of irregular verbs

The past tense and past participle forms of irregular verbs are often confused. The most frequent error is using a past tense form instead of the past participle with *had.*

Incorrect	She had never **rode** (PAST TENSE) a horse before.
Correct	She had never **ridden** (PAST PARTICIPLE) a horse before.
Incorrect	He had **saw** (PAST TENSE) many alligators in Louisiana.
Correct	He had **seen** (PAST PARTICIPLE) many alligators in Louisiana.

Remember: Change any past tense verbs preceded by *had* to past participles.

24c Transitive and Intransitive Verbs

Lay/lie, set/sit, and *raise/rise*

Do your house keys lay or lie on the kitchen table? Does a book set or sit on the shelf? *Raise/rise, lay/lie,* and *set/sit* are transitive/intransitive verb pairs that writers frequently confuse. **Transitive verbs** take direct objects—nouns that receive the action of the verb. **Intransitive verbs** act in sentences that lack direct objects. Chickens *lay* eggs, but people *lie* down.

The following charts list the trickiest pairs of transitive and intransitive verbs and the correct forms for each verb tense. Pay special attention to *lay* and *lie,* which are irregular.

	lay (put something down)	**lie (recline)**
Present	lay, lays	lie, lies
Past participle	laying	lying
Past	laid	lay
Past participle	laid	lain

Transitive When you complete your test, please lay your pencil [direct object, the thing being laid down] on the desk.

Intransitive The *Titanic* lies upright in two pieces at a depth of 13,000 feet.

	raise (elevate something)	**rise (get up)**
Present	raise, raises	rise, rises
Present participle	raising	rising
Past	raised	rose
Past participle	raised	risen

Transitive We raise our glasses [direct object, the things being raised] to toast Uncle Han.

Intransitive The sun rises over the bay.

	set (place something)	**sit (take a seat)**
Present	set, sets	sit, sits
Present participle	setting	sitting
Past	set	sat
Past participle	set	sat

Transitive Every morning Stanley sets two dollars [direct object, the amount being set] on the table to tip the waiter.

Intransitive I sit in the front seat if it's available.

25 Pronouns

QUICK*TAKE*

- Choose the correct pronoun case (see below)
- Identify and correct errors in pronoun agreement (see p. 197)

 Pronoun Case

Subjective pronouns function as the subjects of sentences. **Objective pronouns** function as direct or indirect objects. **Possessive pronouns** indicate ownership.

Subjective pronouns	**Objective pronouns**	**Possessive pronouns**
I	me	my, mine
we	us	our, ours
you	you	your, yours
he	him	his
she	her	her, hers
it	it	its
they	them	their, theirs
who	whom	whose

Pronouns in compound phrases

Picking the right pronoun can sometimes be confusing when the pronoun appears in a compound phrase.

If we work together, you and **me** can get the job done quickly.

If we work together, you and **I** can get the job done quickly.

Which is correct—*me* or *I*? Removing the other pronoun usually makes the choice clear.

Incorrect **Me** can get the job done quickly.

Correct **I** can get the job done quickly.

We and *us* before nouns

Another pair of pronouns that can cause difficulty is *we* and *us* before nouns.

> **Us** friends must stick together.
>
> **We** friends must stick together.

Which is correct—*us* or *we*? Removing the noun indicates the correct choice.

Incorrect	**Us** must stick together.
Correct	**We** must stick together.

Who versus *whom*

Choosing between *who* and *whom* is often difficult, even for experienced writers. The distinction between *who* and *whom* is disappearing from spoken language. *Who* is more often used in spoken language, even when *whom* is correct.

COMMON ERRORS

Who or *whom*

In writing, the distinction between *who* and *whom* is still often observed. *Who* and *whom* follow the same rules as other pronouns: *Who* is the subject pronoun; *whom* is the object pronoun. If you are dealing with an object, *whom* is the correct choice.

Incorrect	**Who** did you send the letter to? **Who** did you give the present to?
Correct	To **whom** did you send the letter? **Whom** did you give the present to?

Who is always the right choice for the subject pronoun.

Correct	**Who** gave you the present? **Who** brought the cookies?

(Continued on next page)

COMMON ERRORS *(Continued)*

If you are uncertain of which one to use, try substituting *she* and *her* or *he* and *him.*

Incorrect You sent the letter to **she [who]**?

Correct You sent the letter to **her [whom]**?

Incorrect **Him [Whom]** gave you the present?

Correct **He [Who]** gave you the present?

Remember: ***Who* = subject**
***Whom* = object**

Whoever versus *whomever*

With the rule regarding *who* and *whom* in mind, you can distinguish between *whoever* and *whomever.* Which is correct?

Her warmth touched **whoever** she met.

Her warmth touched **whomever** she met.

In this sentence, the pronoun functions as the direct object in its own clause: she met whomever. Thus, *whomever* is the correct choice.

Pronouns in comparisons

When you write a sentence using a comparison that includes *than* or *as* followed by a pronoun, usually you will have to think about which pronoun is correct. Which of the following is correct?

Vimala is a faster swimmer than **him.**

Vimala is a faster swimmer than **he.**

The test that will give you the correct answer is to add the verb that finishes the sentence—in this case, *is.*

Incorrect Vimala is a faster swimmer than **him is.**

Correct Vimala is a faster swimmer than **he is.**

Adding the verb makes the correct choice evident.

Possessive pronouns

Possessive pronouns are confusing at times, because possessive nouns are formed with apostrophes, but possessive pronouns do not require apostrophes. Pronouns that use apostrophes are always **contractions**.

It's	=	It is
Who's	=	Who is
They're	=	They are

The test for whether to use an apostrophe is to determine if the pronoun is possessive or a contraction. The most confusing pair is *its* and *it's*.

Incorrect Its a sure thing she will be elected. [Contraction needed]

Correct It's a sure thing she will be elected. [**It is** a sure thing.]

Incorrect The dog lost it's collar. [Possessive needed]

Correct The dog lost its collar.

25b Pronoun Agreement

Because pronouns usually replace or refer to other nouns, they must match those nouns in number and gender. The noun that the pronoun replaces is called its **antecedent**. If pronoun and antecedent match, they are in **agreement**. When a pronoun is close to the antecedent, usually there is no problem.

Maria forgot her coat.

The band **members** collected their uniforms.

Pronoun agreement errors often happen when pronouns and the nouns they replace are separated by several words.

Incorrect

The **players**, exhausted from the double-overtime game, picked up his sweats and walked toward the locker rooms.

Correct

The **players**, exhausted from the double-overtime game, picked up their sweats and walked toward the locker rooms.

Careful writers make sure that pronouns match their antecedents.

COMMON ERRORS

Indefinite pronouns

Indefinite pronouns (such as *anybody, anything, each, either, everybody, everything, neither, none, somebody, something*) refer to unspecified people or things. Most take singular pronouns.

Incorrect Everybody can choose **their** roommates.

Correct Everybody can choose **his or her** roommate.

Correct alternative All students can choose **their** roommates.

A few indefinite pronouns (*all, any, either, more, most, neither, none, some*) can take either singular or plural pronouns.

Correct **Some** of the shipment was damaged when **it** became overheated.

Correct **All** thought **they** should have a good seat at the concert.

A few pronouns are always plural (*few, many, several*).

Correct **Several** want refunds.

Remember: Words that begin with *any*, *some*, and *every* are usually singular.

Collective nouns

Collective nouns (such as *audience, class, committee, crowd, family, herd, jury, team*) can be singular or plural depending on whether the emphasis is on the group or on its individual members.

Correct The **committee** was unanimous in **its** decision.

Correct The **committee** put **their** opinions ahead of the goals of the unit.

COMMON ERRORS

e Edit Help

Pronoun agreement with compound antecedents

Antecedents joined by *and* take plural pronouns.

Correct **Moncef and Driss** practiced their music.

Exception: When compound antecedents are preceded by *each* or *every,* use a singular pronoun.

Correct **Every male cardinal and warbler** arrives before the female to define its territory.

When compound antecedents are connected by *or* or *nor,* the pronoun agrees with the antecedent closer to it.

Incorrect **Either the Ross twins or Angela** should bring their games.

Correct **Either the Ross twins or Angela** should bring her games.

Better **Either Angela or the Ross twins** should bring their games.

When you put the plural *twins* last, the correct choice becomes the plural pronoun *their.*

Remember:

1. **Use plural pronouns for antecedents joined by *and*.**
2. **Use singular pronouns for antecedents preceded by *each* or *every*.**
3. **Use a pronoun that agrees with the nearest antecedent when compound antecedents are joined by *or* or *nor*.**

25c Avoid Sexist Pronouns

English does not have a neutral singular pronoun for a group of mixed genders or a person of unknown gender. Referring to a group of mixed genders using male pronouns is unacceptable to many people. Unless the school in the following example is all male, many readers would object to the use of *his*.

Sexist **Each student** must select **his** courses using the online registration system.

One strategy is to use *her or his* or *his or her* instead of *his.*

Correct **Each student** must select **his or her** courses using the online registration system.

Often you can avoid using *his or her* by changing the noun to the plural form.

Better **All students** must select **their** courses using the online registration system.

In some cases, however, using *his or her* is necessary.

 25d Vague Reference

Pronouns can sometimes refer to more than one noun, thus confusing readers.

> The **coach** rushed past the injured **player** to yell at the **referee.** **She** was hit in the face by a stray elbow.

You have to guess which person *she* refers to—the coach, the player, or the referee. Sometimes you cannot even guess the antecedent of a pronoun.

> The new subdivision destroyed the last remaining habitat for wildlife within the city limits. **They** have ruined our city with their unchecked greed.

Whom does *they* refer to? The mayor and city council? The developers? The people who live in the subdivision? Or all of the above?

Pronouns should never leave the reader guessing about antecedents. If different nouns can be confused as the antecedent, then the ambiguity should be clarified.

Vague Mafalda's pet boa constrictor crawled across Tonya's foot. **She** was mortified.

Better When Mafalda's pet boa constrictor crawled across Tonya's foot, **Mafalda** was mortified.

COMMON ERRORS

Vague use of *this*

Always use a noun immediately after *this, that, these, those,* and *some.*

Vague Enrique asked Meg to remove the viruses on his computer. **This** was a bad idea.

Was it a bad idea for Enrique to ask Meg because she was insulted? Because she didn't know how? Because removing viruses would destroy some of Enrique's files?

Better Enrique asked Meg to remove the viruses on his computer. **This imposition** on Meg's time was a bad idea.

Remember: Ask yourself "this *what?*" and add the noun that *this* refers to.

26 Shifts

QUICK*TAKE*

- Identify and correct verb tense shifts (see below)
- Identify and correct shifts in mood (see p. 203), voice (see p. 204), and person and number (see p. 204)

26a Shifts in Tense

Appropriate shifts in verb tense

Changes in verb tense are sometimes necessary to indicate a shift in time.

Past to future Because Oda **won** (PAST TENSE) the lottery, she **will quit** (FUTURE TENSE) her job at the hospital as soon as her supervisor **finds** (PRESENT TENSE) a qualified replacement.

Inappropriate shifts in verb tense

Be careful to avoid confusing your reader with shifts in verb tense.

Incorrect

PRESENT TENSE
While Brazil **looks** to ecotourism to fund rain forest
PAST TENSE
preservation, other South American nations **relied** on
foreign aid and conservation efforts.

The shift from present tense (*looks*) to past tense (*relied*) is confusing. Correct the mistake by putting both verbs in the present tense.

Correct

PRESENT TENSE
While Brazil **looks** to ecotourism to fund rain forest
PRESENT TENSE
preservation, other South American nations **rely** on
foreign aid and conservation efforts.

COMMON ERRORS

Unnecessary tense shift

Notice the tense shift in the following example.

Incorrect

PAST TENSE
In May of 2000 the "I Love You" virus **crippled** the
computer systems of major American companies and
PAST TENSE
irritated millions of private computer users. As the
PRESENT TENSE / PRESENT TENSE
virus **generates** millions of e-mails and **erases** millions
of computer files, companies such as Ford and Time
PRESENT TENSE
Warner **are** forced to shut down their clogged e-mail
systems.

The second sentence shifts unnecessarily to the present tense, confusing the reader. Did the "I Love You" virus have its heyday several years ago, or is it still wreaking havoc now? Changing the verbs in the second sentence to the past tense eliminates the confusion.

COMMON ERRORS

Correct In May of 2000 the "I Love You" virus crippled (PAST TENSE) the computer systems of major American companies and irritated (PAST TENSE) millions of private computer users. As the virus generated (PAST TENSE) millions of e-mails and erased (PAST TENSE) millions of computer files, companies such as Ford and Time Warner were (PAST TENSE) forced to shut down their clogged e-mail systems.

Remember: Shift verb tense only when you are referring to different time periods.

 26b Shifts in Mood

Verbs can be categorized into three moods—indicative, imperative, and subjunctive—defined by the functions they serve.

Indicative verbs state facts, opinions, and questions.

Fact Many same-sex couples in the United States are fighting for the right to marry.

Imperative verbs make commands, give advice, and make requests.

Command Tell me why you support same-sex marriage.

Subjunctive verbs express wishes, unlikely or untrue situations, hypothetical situations, requests with *that* clauses, and suggestions.

Unlikely or untrue situation If heterosexual marriage were as sacred as some pundits would have us believe, there would be no divorce.

Be careful not to shift from one mood to another in midsentence.

Incorrect If the government **were** to shift funding priorities away from earthquake research, scientists lose even more time in understanding how to predict earthquakes.

The sudden shift from subjunctive to indicative mood in this sentence is confusing. Are the scientists losing time now, or is losing time a likely result of a government funding shift? Revise the sentence to keep both verbs in the subjunctive.

Correct If the government **were** to shift funding priorities away from earthquake research, scientists **would lose** even more time in understanding how to predict earthquakes.

26c Shifts in Voice

Watch for unintended shifts from active (*I ate the cookies*) to passive voice (*the cookies were eaten*).

Incorrect The sudden storm **toppled** several trees, and numerous windows **were shattered.**

The unexpected shift from active voice (*toppled*) to passive (*were shattered*) forces readers to wonder whether it was the sudden storm, or something else, that broke the windows.

Correct The sudden storm **toppled** several trees and **shattered** numerous windows.

Revising the sentence to eliminate the shift to passive voice (see Section 18a) also creates a parallel structure (see Section 20c).

26d Shifts in Person and Number

Sudden shifts from third person (*he, she, it, one*) to first (*I, we*) or second (*you*) are confusing to readers and often indicate a writer's uncertainty about how to address a reader. We often make such shifts in spoken English, but in formal writing, shifts in person need to be recognized and corrected.

Incorrect When **one** is reading a magazine, **you** often see several different type fonts used on a single page.

The shift from third person to second person in this sentence is confusing.

Correct When reading a magazine, **you** often see several different type fonts used on a single page.

Similarly, shifts from singular to plural subjects (see Section 23b) within a single sentence confuse readers.

27 Modifiers

QUICK*TAKE*

- Use the correct form of comparatives and superlatives (see below)
- Identify and correct dangling modifiers (see p. 210)

27a Choose the Correct Modifier

Modifiers come in two varieties: adjectives and adverbs. The same words can function as adjectives or adverbs, depending on what they modify.

Adjectives modify

nouns—*iced* tea, *power* forward
pronouns—He is *brash*.

Adverbs modify

verbs—*barely* reach, drive *carefully*
adjectives—*truly* brave activist, *shockingly* red lipstick
other adverbs—*not* soon forget, *very* well
clauses—*Honestly,* I find ballet boring.

Adjectives answer the questions *Which one? How many?* and *What kind?* Adverbs answer the questions *How often? To what extent? When? Where? How?* and *Why?*

Use the correct forms of comparatives and superlatives

Comparative modifiers weigh one thing against another. They either end in *-er* or are preceded by *more*.

Road bikes are **faster** on pavement than mountain bikes.

The **more courageous** juggler tossed flaming torches.

Superlative modifiers compare three or more items. They either end in *-est* or are preceded by *most.*

April is the **hottest** month in New Delhi.

Wounded animals are the **most ferocious**.

Some frequently used comparatives and superlatives are irregular. The following list can help you become familiar with them.

Adjective	**Comparative**	**Superlative**
good	better	best
bad	worse	worst
little (amount)	less	least
many, much	more	most
Adverb	**Comparative**	**Superlative**
well	better	best
badly	worse	worst

Do not use both a suffix (*-er* or *-est*) and *more* or *most.*

Incorrect The service at Jane's Restaurant is **more slower** than the service at Alphonso's.

Correct The service at Jane's Restaurant is **slower** than the service at Alphonso's.

Absolute modifiers are words that represent an unvarying condition and thus aren't subject to the degrees that comparative and superlative constructions convey. Common absolute modifiers include *complete, ultimate,* and *unique. Unique,* for example, means "one of a kind." There's nothing else like it. Thus, something cannot be *very unique* or *totally unique.* It is either unique or it isn't. Absolute modifiers should not be modified by comparatives (*more* + modifier or modifier + *er*) or superlatives (*most* + modifier or modifier + *est*).

Double negatives

In English, as in mathematics, two negatives equal a positive. Avoid using two negative words in one sentence, or you'll end up saying the opposite of what you mean. The following are negative words that you should avoid doubling up.

barely	nobody	nothing
hardly	none	scarcely
neither	no one	

Incorrect, double negative	Barely no one noticed that the pop star lip-synched during the whole performance.
Correct, single negative	Barely anyone noticed that the pop star lip-synched during the whole performance.
Incorrect, double negative	When the pastor asked if anyone had objections to the marriage, nobody said nothing.
Correct, single negative	When the pastor asked if anyone had objections to the marriage, nobody said anything.

27b Place Adjectives Carefully

As a general rule, the closer you place a modifier to the word it modifies, the less chance that you will confuse your reader.

Confusing	Watching from the ground below, the kettle of broadwing hawks circled high above the observers.

Is the kettle of hawks watching from the ground below? You can fix the problem by putting the modified subject immediately after the modifier or by placing the modifier next to the modified subject.

Better	The kettle of broadwing hawks circled high above the **observers** who were watching from the ground below.
Better	Watching from the ground below, the **observers** saw a kettle of broadwing hawks circle high above them.

27c Place Adverbs Carefully

Single-word adverbs and adverbial clauses and phrases can usually sit comfortably either before or after the words they modify.

> Dimitri quietly **walked** down the hall.
>
> Dimitri **walked** quietly down the hall.

Conjunctive adverbs—*also, however, instead, likewise, then, therefore, thus,* and others—are adverbs that show how ideas relate to one another. They prepare a reader for contrasts, exceptions, additions, conclusions, and other shifts in an argument. Conjunctive adverbs can usually fit well into more than one place in the sentence. In the following example, *however* could fit in three different places.

Between two main clauses

> Professional football players earn exorbitant salaries; however, they pay for their wealth with lifetimes of chronic pain and debilitating injuries.

Within second main clause

> Professional football players earn exorbitant salaries; they pay for their wealth, however, with lifetimes of chronic pain and debilitating injuries.

At end of second main clause

> Professional football players earn exorbitant salaries; they pay for their wealth with lifetimes of chronic pain and debilitating injuries, however.

COMMON ERRORS

Placement of limiting modifiers

Words such as *almost, even, hardly, just, merely, nearly, not, only,* and *simply* are called **limiting modifiers.** Although people often are careless with their placement in everyday speech, limiting modifiers should always go immediately before the word or words they modify in your writing. Like other limiting modifiers, *only* should be placed immediately before the word it modifies.

Incorrect The Gross National Product only gives one indicator of economic growth.

Correct The Gross National Product gives only one indicator of economic growth.

The word *only* modifies *one* in this sentence, not *Gross National Product.*

Remember: Place limiting modifiers immediately before the word(s) they modify.

27d Hyphens with Compound Modifiers

When to hyphenate

Hyphenate a compound modifier that precedes a noun.

When a compound modifier precedes a noun, you should usually hyphenate the modifier. A **compound modifier** consists of words that join together as a unit to modify a noun.

middle-class values self-fulfilling prophecy

Hyphenate a phrase when it is used as a modifier that precedes a noun.

all-you-can-eat buffet step-by-step instructions

Hyphenate the prefixes *pro-*, *anti-*, *post-*, *pre-*, *neo-*, and *mid-* before proper nouns.

neo-Nazi racism mid-Atlantic states

Hyphenate a compound modifier with a number when it precedes a noun.

eighteenth-century drama one-way street

When not to hyphenate

Do not hyphenate a compound modifier that follows a noun.

The instructor's approach is student centered.

Do not hyphenate compound modifiers when the first word is *very* or ends in *ly*.

newly recorded data very cold day

27e Revise Dangling Modifiers

Some modifiers are ambiguous because they could apply to more than one word or clause. Dangling modifiers are ambiguous for the opposite reason; they don't have a word to modify. In such cases, the modifier is usually an introductory clause or phrase. What is being modified should immediately follow the phrase, but in the following sentence, it is absent.

After bowling a perfect game, Surfside Lanes hung Marco's photo on the wall.

You can eliminate a dangling modifier in two ways:

1. Insert the noun or pronoun being modified immediately after the introductory modifying phrase.

   After bowling a perfect game, Marco was honored by having his photo hung on the wall at Surfside Lanes.

2. Rewrite the introductory phrase as an introductory clause to include the noun or pronoun.

   After **Marco** bowled a perfect game, Surfside Lanes hung his photo on the wall.

COMMON ERRORS

Dangling modifiers

A dangling modifier does not seem to modify anything in a sentence; it dangles, unconnected to the word or words it presumably is intended to modify. Frequently, it produces funny results.

Incorrect **When still a girl,** my father joined the army.

It sounds like *father* was once a girl. The problem is that the subject, *I,* is missing.

Correct **When I was still a girl,** my father joined the army.

Remember: Modifiers should be clearly connected to the words they modify, especially at the beginning of sentences.

28 Grammar for Multilingual Writers

QUICK*TAKE*

- Understand the types of English nouns (see below)
- Use articles correctly (see p. 213)
- Use verbs correctly (see p. 214)

 28a Nouns

Perhaps the most troublesome conventions for nonnative speakers are those that guide usage of the common articles *the, a,* and *an*. To understand how articles work in English, you must first understand how the language uses **nouns**.

Kinds of nouns

There are two basic kinds of nouns. A **proper noun** begins with a capital letter and names a unique person, place, or thing: *Theodore Roosevelt, Russia, Eiffel Tower.*

The other basic kind of noun is called a **common noun**. Common nouns do not name a unique person, place, or thing: *man, country, tower.*

Count and noncount nouns

Common nouns can be classified as either *count* or *noncount*. **Count nouns** can be made plural, usually by adding *-s* (*finger, fingers*) or by using their plural forms (*person, people; datum, data*). **Noncount nouns** cannot be counted directly and cannot take the plural form (*information,* but not *informations; garbage,* but not *garbages*). Some nouns can be either count or noncount, depending on how they are used. *Hair* can refer to either a strand of hair, where it serves as a count noun, or a mass of hair, where it becomes a noncount noun.

COMMON ESL ERRORS

Singular and plural forms of count nouns

Count nouns are simpler to quantify than noncount nouns. But remember that English requires you to state both singular and plural forms of nouns explicitly. Look at the following sentences.

Incorrect The three bicyclist shaved their leg before the big race.

Correct The three bicyclists shaved their legs before the big race.

Remember: English requires you to use plural forms of count nouns even if a plural number is otherwise indicated.

28b Articles

Articles indicate that a noun is about to appear, and they clarify what the noun refers to. There are only two kinds of articles in English, definite and indefinite:

1. **the:** *The* is a **definite article**, meaning that it refers to (1) a specific object already known to the reader, (2) one about to be made known to the reader, or (3) a unique object.
2. **a, an:** The **indefinite articles** *a* and *an* refer to an object whose specific identity is not known to the reader. The only difference between *a* and *an* is that *a* is used before a consonant sound (*man, friend, yellow*), while *an* is used before a vowel sound (*animal, enemy, orange*).

COMMON ESL ERRORS

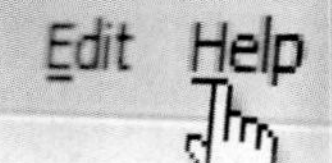

Articles with count and noncount nouns

Knowing how to distinguish between count and noncount nouns can help you decide which article to use. Noncount nouns are never used with the indefinite articles *a* or *an*.

Incorrect Maria jumped into **a** water.

Correct Maria jumped into **the** water.

No articles are used with noncount and plural count nouns when you wish to state something that has a general application.

Incorrect **The** water is a precious natural resource.

Correct Water is a precious natural resource.

Remember:

1. **Noncount nouns are never used with *a* and *an*.**
2. **Noncount and plural nouns used to make general statements do not take articles.**

28c Verbs

The verb system in English can be divided between simple verbs like *run, speak,* and *look,* and verb phrases like *may have run, have spoken,* and *will be looking*. In these examples, the words that appear before the main verbs—*may, have, will,* and *be*—are called **auxiliary verbs** (also called **helping verbs**).

Indicating tense and voice with *be* verbs

Like the other auxiliary verbs *have* and *do, be* changes form to signal tense. In addition to *be* itself, the **be verbs** are *is, am, are, was, were,* and *been*. To show ongoing action, *be* verbs are followed by the present participle, which is a verb with an *-ing* ending.

Incorrect I **am think** of all the things I'd rather **be do**.

Correct I **am thinking** of all the things I'd rather **be doing**.

To show that an action is being done to, rather than by, the subject, follow *be* verbs with the past participle (a verb usually ending in *-ed, -en,* or *-t*).

Incorrect The movie **was direct** by John Woo.

Correct The movie **was directed** by John Woo.

Modal auxiliary verbs

Modal auxiliary verbs *will, would, can, could, may, might, shall, must,* and *should* express conditions like possibility, permission, speculation, expectation, obligation, and necessity. Unlike the auxiliary verbs *be, have,* and *do,* modal verbs do not change form based on the grammatical subject of the sentence (*I, you, she, he, it, we, they*).

Two basic rules apply to all uses of modal verbs. First, modal verbs are always followed by the simple form of the verb. The simple form is the verb by itself, in the present tense, such as *have* but not *had, having,* or *to have*.

Incorrect She should **studies** harder to pass the exam.

Correct She should **study** harder to pass the exam.

The second rule is that you should not use modals consecutively.

Incorrect If you work harder at writing, you **might could** improve.

Correct If you work harder at writing, you **might** improve.

Phrasal verbs

The liveliest and most colorful feature of the English language, its numerous idiomatic verbal phrases, gives many multilingual speakers the greatest difficulty.

Phrasal verbs consist of a verb and one or two **particles**: either a preposition, an adverb, or both. The verb and particles combine to form a phrase with a particular meaning that is often quite distinct from the meaning of the verb itself. Consider the following sentence.

I need to **go over** the chapter once more before the test.

Here, the meaning of *go over*—a verb and a preposition that, taken together, suggest casual study—is only weakly related to the meaning of either *go* or *over* by itself. English has hundreds of such idiomatic constructions, and the best way to familiarize yourself with them is to listen to and read as much informal English as you can.

Like regular verbs, phrasal verbs can be either transitive (they take a direct object) or intransitive. In the preceding example, *go over* is transitive. *Quiet down*—as in *Please quiet down*—is intransitive. Some phrases, like *wake up*, can be both: *Wake up!* is intransitive, while *Jenny, wake up the children* is transitive.

In some transitive phrasal verbs, the particles can be separated from the verb without affecting the meaning: *I made up a song* is equivalent to *I made a song up*. In others, the particles cannot be separated from the verb.

Incorrect You shouldn't **play** with love **around**.

Correct You shouldn't **play around** with love.

Unfortunately, there are no shortcuts for learning which verbal phrases are separable and which are not. As you become increasingly familiar with English, you will grow more confident in your ability to use phrasal verbs.

If you are unsure about a phrasal verb, type it in *Google* or another search engine with quotation marks around it. The results of the search will tell you if it is an idiomatic English construction.

PART 6 Understanding Punctuation and Mechanics

29 Commas

QUICK*TAKE*

- Set off parts of sentences with commas (see below)
- Use commas correctly with quotations (see p. 225)
- Avoid unnecessary commas (see p. 227)

29a Commas with Introductory Elements

Introductory elements usually need to be set off by commas. When a conjunctive adverb (see Section 27c) or introductory phrase begins a sentence, the comma follows.

> **Therefore,** the suspect could not have been at the scene of the crime.
>
> **Above all,** remember to let water drip from the faucets if the temperature drops below freezing.

When a conjunctive adverb comes in the middle of a sentence, set it off with commas preceding and following.

> If you really want to prevent your pipes from freezing, **however,** you should insulate them before the winter comes.

Occasionally the conjunctive adverb or phrase blends into a sentence so smoothly that a pause would sound awkward.

Awkward	Even if you take every precaution, the pipes in your home may freeze, **nevertheless**.
Better	Even if you take every precaution, the pipes in your home may freeze **nevertheless**.

COMMON ERRORS

Edit Help

Commas with long introductory modifiers

Long subordinate clauses or phrases that begin sentences should be followed by a comma. The following sentence lacks the needed comma.

Incorrect Because teens and younger adults are so comfortable with and reliant on smartphones texting while driving does not immediately seem like an irresponsible and possibly deadly act.

When you read this sentence, you likely had to go back to sort it out. The words *smartphones* and *texting* tend to run together. When the comma is added, the sentence is easier to understand because the reader knows where the subordinate clause ends and where the main clause begins.

Correct Because teens and younger adults are so comfortable with and reliant on smartphones, texting while driving does not immediately seem like an irresponsible and possibly deadly act.

How long is a long introductory modifier? Short introductory adverbial phrases and clauses of five words or fewer can get by without the comma if the omission does not mislead the reader. Using the comma is still correct after short introductory adverbial phrases and clauses.

Correct In the long run stocks have always done better than bonds.

Correct In the long run, stocks have always done better than bonds.

Remember: Put commas after long introductory modifiers.

29b Commas with Compound Clauses

Two main clauses joined by a coordinating conjunction (*and, or, so, yet, but, nor, for*) form a compound sentence. Writers sometimes get confused about when to insert a comma before a coordinating conjunction.

Use a comma and a coordinating conjunction to separate main clauses

Main clauses carry enough grammatical weight to be punctuated as sentences. When two main clauses are joined by a coordinating conjunction, place a comma before the coordinating conjunction in order to distinguish them.

> Sandy borrowed Martin's iPad on Tuesday, **and** she returned it on Friday.

Very short main clauses joined by a coordinating conjunction do not need commas.

> She called **and** she called, but no one answered.

Do not use a comma to separate two verbs with the same subject

Incorrect Sandy borrowed Martin's video camera on Tuesday, and returned it on Friday.

Sandy is the subject of both *borrowed* and *returned.* This sentence has only one main clause; it should not be punctuated as a compound sentence.

Correct Sandy borrowed Martin's video camera on Tuesday and returned it on Friday.

Do not use a comma to searate a main clause from a restrictive clause or phrase

When clauses and phrases that follow the main clause are essential to the meaning of a sentence, they should not be set off with a comma.

Incorrect Sandy plans to borrow Felicia's DVD collection, while Felicia is on vacation.

Correct Sandy plans to borrow Felicia's DVD collection while Felicia is on vacation.

COMMON ERRORS

Commas in compound sentences

The easiest way to distinguish between compound sentences and sentences with phrases that follow the main clause is to isolate the part that comes after the conjunction. If the part that follows the conjunction can stand on its own as a complete sentence, insert a comma. If it cannot, omit the comma.

Main clause plus phrases

Mario thinks he lost his passport while riding the bus or by absentmindedly leaving it on the counter when he checked into the hostel.

Look at what comes after the coordinating conjunction *or.*

by absentmindedly leaving it on the counter when he checked into the hostel

This group of words is not a main clause and cannot stand on its own as a complete sentence. Do not set it off with a comma.

Main clauses joined with a conjunction

On Saturday Mario went to the American consulate to get a new passport, but the officer told him that replacement passports could not be issued on weekends.

Read the clause after the coordinating conjunction *but.*

the officer told him that replacement passports could not be issued on weekends

This group of words can stand on its own as a complete sentence. Thus, it is a main clause; place a comma before *but.*

Remember:

1. **Place a comma before the coordinating conjunction (*and, but, for, or, nor, so, yet*) when there are two main clauses.**
2. **Do not use a comma before the coordinating conjunction when there is only one main clause.**

COMMON ERRORS

Do not use a comma to set off a *because* clause that follows a main clause

Writers frequently place unnecessary commas before *because* and similar subordinate conjunctions that follow a main clause. *Because* is not a coordinating conjunction; thus it should not be set off by a comma unless the comma improves readability.

Incorrect I struggled to complete my term papers last year, because I worked at two jobs.

Correct I struggled to complete my term papers last year because I worked at two jobs.

But do use a comma after an introductory *because* clause.

Incorrect Because Danny left his red jersey at home Coach Russell benched him.

Correct Because Danny left his red jersey at home, Coach Russell benched him.

Remember: Use a comma after a *because* clause that begins a sentence. Do not use a comma to set off a *because* clause that follows a main clause.

29c Commas with Nonrestrictive Modifiers

Imagine that you are sending a friend a group photo that includes your aunt. Which sentence is correct?

In the back row the woman wearing the pink hat is my aunt.

In the back row the woman, wearing the pink hat, is my aunt.

Both sentences can be correct depending on what is in the photo. If there are three women standing in the back row and only one is wearing a pink hat, this piece of information is necessary for identifying your aunt. In this

case the sentence without commas is correct because it identifies your aunt as the woman wearing the pink hat. Such necessary modifiers are **restrictive** and do not require commas.

If only one woman is standing in the back row, *wearing the pink hat* is extra information and not necessary to identify your aunt. The modifier in this case is **nonrestrictive** and is set off by commas.

Distinguish restrictive and nonrestrictive modifiers

You can distinguish between restrictive and nonrestrictive modifiers by deleting the modifier and then deciding whether the essential meaning of the sentence is changed. For example, delete the modifier *still stained by its bloody Tianamen Square crackdown* from the following sentence.

> Some members of the Olympic Site Selection Committee wanted to prevent China, **still stained by its bloody Tianamen Square crackdown,** from hosting the 2008 games.

The result leaves the meaning of the main clause unchanged.

> Some members of the Olympic Site Selection Committee wanted to prevent China from hosting the 2008 games.

The modifier is nonrestrictive and should be set off by commas.

Pay special attention to appositives

Clauses and phrases can be restrictive or nonrestrictive, depending on the context. Often the difference is obvious, but some modifiers require close consideration, especially appositives. An **appositive** is a noun or noun phrase that identifies or adds information to the noun preceding it.

Consider the following pair.

1 Apple's tablet computer the iPad introduced a class of devices between smartphones and laptops.

2 Apple's tablet computer, the iPad, introduced a class of devices between smartphones and laptops.

Which is correct? The appositive *the iPad* is not essential to the meaning of the sentence and simply offers additional information. Sentence 2 is correct.

Use commas to mark off parenthetical expressions

A **parenthetical expression** provides information or commentary that usually is not essential to the sentence's meaning.

Incorrect My mother much to my surprise didn't say anything when she saw my pierced nose.

Correct My mother, much to my surprise, didn't say anything when she saw my pierced nose.

29d Commas with Items in a Series

In a series of three or more items, place a comma after each item except the last one. The comma between the last two items goes before the conjunction (*and, or*).

> Health officials in Trenton, Manhattan, and the Bronx have all reported new cases of the West Nile virus.

29e Commas with Coordinate Adjectives

Coordinate adjectives are two or more adjectives that modify the same noun independently. Coordinate adjectives that are not linked by *and* must be separated by a comma.

> After the financial crisis of 2007–2010, the creators of credit-default swaps and other risky investments are no longer the **fresh-faced, giddy** kids of Wall Street.

You can recognize coordinate adjectives by reversing their order; if their meaning remains the same, the adjectives are coordinate and must be linked by *and* or separated by a comma.

Commas are not used between **cumulative adjectives**. Cumulative adjectives are two or more adjectives that work together to modify a noun: *deep blue sea, inexpensive mountain bike*. If reversing their order changes the description of the noun (or violates the order of English, such as *mountain inexpensive bike*), the adjectives are cumulative and should not be separated by a comma.

29f Commas with Quotations

Properly punctuating quotations with commas can be tricky unless you know a few rules about when and where to use commas.

When to use commas with quotations

Commas set off signal phrases that attribute quotations to a speaker or writer, such as *he argues, they said,* and *she writes.*

> "When you come to a fork in the road," said Yogi Berra, "take it!"

If the signal phrase follows a quotation that is a complete sentence, replace the period that would normally come at the end of the quotation with a comma.

Incorrect "Simplicity of language is not only reputable but perhaps even sacred." writes Kurt Vonnegut.

Correct "Simplicity of language is not only reputable but perhaps even sacred," writes Kurt Vonnegut.

When not to use commas with quotations

Do not replace a question mark or exclamation point with a comma.

Incorrect "Who's on first," Costello asked Abbott.

Correct "Who's on first?" Costello asked Abbott.

Not all phrases that mention the author's name are signal phrases. When quoting a term or using a quotation within a subordinate clause, do not set off the quotation with commas.

> "Stonewall" Jackson gained his nickname at the First Battle of Bull Run when General Barnard Bee shouted to his men that Jackson was "standing like a stone wall."

 Commas with Dates, Numbers, Titles, and Addresses

Some of the easiest comma rules to remember are the ones we use every day in dates, numbers, personal titles, place names, direct address, and brief interjections.

Commas with dates

Use commas to separate the day of the week from the month and to set off a year from the rest of the sentence.

> Monday, November 17, 2014
>
> On July 27, 2015, the opening ceremony of the World Scout Jamboree will be televised.

Do not use a comma when the month immediately precedes the year.

> April 2016

Commas with numbers

Commas mark off thousands, millions, billions, and so on.

> 16,500,000

However, do not use commas in street addresses or page numbers.

> page 1542
>
> 7602 Elm Street

Commas with personal titles

When a title follows a person's name, set the title off with commas.

> Zoe Hart, MD

Commas with place names

Place a comma between street addresses, city names, state names, and countries but not before zip codes.

> Write to the president at 1600 Pennsylvania Avenue, Washington, DC 20500.

Commas with brief interjections

Use commas to set off brief interjections like *yes* and *no,* as well as short questions that fall at the ends of sentences.

> Have another piece of pie, won't you?

29h Commas to Avoid Confusion

Certain sentences can be confusing if you do not indicate where readers should pause within the sentence. Use a comma to guide a reader through these usually compact constructions.

> **Unclear** With supplies low prices of gasoline and fuel oil will increase.

This sentence could be read as meaning *With supplies, low prices will increase.*

> **Clear** With supplies low, prices of gasoline and fuel oil will increase.

29i Unnecessary Commas

Do not place a comma between a subject and the main verb.

> **Incorrect** American children of immigrant parents, often do not speak their parents' native language.

> **Correct** American children of immigrant parents often do not speak their parents' native language.

However, do use commas to set off modifying phrases that separate subjects from verbs.

> **Correct** Steven Pinker, author of *The Language Instinct,* argues that the ability to speak and understand language is an evolutionary adaptive trait.

Do not use a comma with a coordinating conjunction unless it joins two main clauses. (See the Common Errors box on page 221.)

Incorrect Susana thought finishing her first novel was hard, but soon learned that getting a publisher to buy it was much harder.

Correct Susana thought finishing her first novel was hard but soon learned that getting a publisher to buy it was much harder.

Correct Susana thought finishing her first novel was hard, but **she** soon learned that getting a publisher to buy it was much harder.

Do not use a comma after a subordinating conjunction such as *although, despite,* or *while.*

Incorrect Although, soccer is gaining popularity in the States, it will never be as popular as football or baseball.

Correct Although soccer is gaining popularity in the States, it will never be as popular as football or baseball.

Some writers mistakenly use a comma with *than* to try to heighten the contrast in a comparison.

Incorrect Any teacher will tell you that acquiring critical thinking skills is more important, than simply memorizing information.

Correct Any teacher will tell you that acquiring critical thinking skills is more important than simply memorizing information.

A common mistake is to place a comma after *such as* or *like* before introducing a list.

Incorrect Many hourly workers, such as, waiters, dishwashers, and cashiers, do not receive health benefits from their employers.

Correct Many hourly workers, such as waiters, dishwashers, and cashiers, do not receive health benefits from their employers.

30 Semicolons and Colons

QUICK*TAKE*

- Use semicolons to link related ideas (see below)
- Use colons correctly in sentences and lists (see pp. 231–233)

30a Semicolons with Closely Related Main Clauses

Why use semicolons? Sometimes we want to join two main clauses to form a complete sentence in order to indicate a relationship and avoid wordiness. We can connect them with a comma and a coordinating conjunction like *or, but,* or *and.* To create variation in sentence style and show a closer relationship, we can omit the comma and coordinating conjunction and insert a semicolon between the two clauses.

Semicolons can join only clauses that are grammatically equal. In other words, they join main clauses only to other main clauses, not to phrases or subordinate clauses. Look at the following examples.

Incorrect [MAIN CLAUSE] Gloria's new weightlifting program will help her recover from knee surgery; [PHRASE] doing a series of squats and presses with a physical therapist.

Correct [MAIN CLAUSE] Gloria's new weightlifting program will help her recover from knee surgery; [MAIN CLAUSE] a physical therapist leads her through a series of squats and presses.

COMMON ERRORS

Semicolons with transitional words and phrases

Closely related main clauses sometimes use a conjunctive adverb (such as *however, therefore, moreover, furthermore, thus, meanwhile, nonetheless, otherwise*) or a transitional phrase (*in fact, for example, that is, for instance, in addition, in other words, on the other hand, even so*) to indicate the relationship between them. When the second clause begins with a conjunctive adverb or a transitional phrase, a semicolon is needed to join the two clauses. This sentence pattern is frequently used; therefore, it pays to learn how to punctuate it correctly.

Incorrect (comma splice) No one doubts that exercise burns calories, however, few people can lose weight by exercise alone.

Correct No one doubts that exercise burns calories; however, few people can lose weight by exercise alone.

Remember: Two main clauses joined by a conjunctive adverb or a transitional phrase require a semicolon.

Do not use a semicolon to introduce quotations

Use a comma or colon instead.

Incorrect Abraham Lincoln often responded to his critics with humor; "If I were two-faced, would I be wearing this one?"

Correct Abraham Lincoln often responded to his critics with humor: "If I were two-faced, would I be wearing this one?"

Do not use a semicolon to introduce lists

Incorrect William Shakespeare wrote four romance plays at the end of his career; *The Tempest, The Winter's Tale, Cymbeline,* and *Pericles*.

Correct William Shakespeare wrote four romance plays at the end of his career: *The Tempest, The Winter's Tale, Cymbeline,* and *Pericles*.

30b Semicolons Together with Commas

When an item in a series already includes a comma, adding more commas to separate it from the other items will only confuse the reader. Use semicolons instead of commas between items in a series that has internal punctuation.

Confusing The church's design competition drew entries from as far away as Gothenberg, Sweden, Caracas, Venezuela, and Athens, Greece.

Clearer The church's design competition drew entries from as far away as Gothenberg, Sweden; Caracas, Venezuela; and Athens, Greece.

Colons in Sentences

Like semicolons, colons can join two closely related main clauses (complete sentences). A colon indicates that what follows will explain or expand on what comes before the colon. Use a colon in cases where the second main clause interprets or sums up the first.

> Anthrozoology, the study of how animals and people relate to one another, sheds light on larger issues in human psychology: people's interactions with animals illustrate concepts of altruism, ethics, and taboo.

You may choose to capitalize the first word of the main clause following the colon or leave it lowercase. Either is correct as long as you are consistent throughout your text.

Colons linking main clauses with appositives

A colon calls attention to an appositive, a noun, or a noun phrase that renames the noun preceding it. If you're not certain whether a colon would be appropriate, put *namely* in its place. If *namely* makes sense when you read the main clause followed by the appositive, you probably need to insert a colon instead of a comma. Remember, the clause that precedes the colon must be a complete sentence.

> I know the perfect person for the job, namely me.

The sentence makes sense with *namely* placed before the appositive. Thus, a colon is appropriate.

> I know the perfect person for the job: me.

Never capitalize a word following a colon unless the word starts a complete sentence or is normally capitalized.

Colons joining main clauses with quotations

Use a colon to link a main clause and a quotation that interprets or sums up the clause. Be careful not to use a colon to link a phrase with a quotation.

Incorrect: phrase–colon–quotation

> President Roosevelt's strategy to change the nation's panicky attitude during the Great Depression: "[T]he only thing we have to fear," he said, "is fear itself."

Correct: main clause–colon–quotation

> President Roosevelt's strategy to end the Great Depression was to change the nation's panicky attitude: "[T]he only thing we have to fear," he said, "is fear itself."

The first example is incorrect because there is no main verb in the first part of the sentence and thus it is a phrase rather than a main clause. The second example adds the verb (*was*), making the first part of the sentence a main clause.

 30d Colons with Lists

Use a colon to join a main clause to a list. The main clauses in these cases sometimes include the phrase *the following* or *as follows*. Remember that a colon cannot join a phrase or an incomplete clause to a list.

Incorrect: phrase–colon–list

> Three ingredients for soup: chicken stock, peeled shrimp, and chopped tomatoes.

Correct: main clause–colon–list

> You can make a tasty soup with just three ingredients: chicken stock, peeled shrimp, and chopped tomatoes.

COMMON ERRORS

Colons misused with lists

Some writers think that anytime they introduce a list, they should insert a colon. Colons are used correctly only when a complete sentence precedes the colon.

Incorrect Jessica's entire wardrobe for her trip to Cancun included: two swimsuits, one pair of shorts, two T-shirts, a party dress, and a pair of sandals.

Correct Jessica's entire wardrobe for her trip to Cancun included two swimsuits, one pair of shorts, two T-shirts, a party dress, and a pair of sandals.

Correct Jessica jotted down what she would need for her trip: two swimsuits, one pair of shorts, two T-shirts, a party dress, and a pair of sandals.

Remember: A colon should be placed only after a clause that can stand by itself as a sentence.

31 Dashes and Parentheses

QUICK*TAKE*

- Use dashes and parentheses rather than commas to set off information (see below)
- Use other punctuation correctly with parentheses (see p. 236)

31a Dashes and Parentheses to Set Off Information

Dashes and parentheses call attention to groups of words. In effect, they tell the reader that a group of words is not part of the main clause and should be given special attention. If you want to make an element stand

out, especially in the middle of a sentence, use parentheses or dashes instead of commas.

Dashes with final elements

A dash is often used to set off a phrase or subordinate clause at the end of a sentence to offer a significant comment about the main clause. Dashes can also anticipate a shift in tone at the end of a sentence.

> A full-sized SUV can take you wherever you want to go in style—if your idea of style is a gas-guzzling tank.

Parentheses with additional information

Parentheses are more often used for identifying information, afterthoughts or asides, examples, and clarification. You can place full sentences, fragments, or brief terms within parentheses.

> Some argue that ethanol (the pet solution of politicians for achieving energy independence) consumes more energy to manufacture and ship than it produces.

COMMON ERRORS

Do not use dashes as periods

Do not use dashes to separate two main clauses (clauses that can stand as complete sentences). Use dashes to separate main clauses from subordinate clauses and phrases when you want to emphasize the subordinate clause or phrase.

> **Incorrect: main clause–dash–main clause**
> I was one of the few women in my computer science classes—most of the students majoring in computer science at that time were men.

> **Correct: main clause–dash–phrase**
> I was one of the few women in computer science—a field then dominated by men.

Remember: Dashes are not periods and should not be used as periods.

31b Dashes and Parentheses Versus Commas

Like commas, parentheses and dashes enclose material that adds, explains, or digresses. However, the three punctuation marks are not interchangeable. The mark you choose depends on how much emphasis you want to place on the material. Dashes indicate the most emphasis. Parentheses offer somewhat less, and commas offer less still.

Commas indicate a moderate level of emphasis

> Bill covered the new tattoo, a pouncing tiger, on his bicep because he thought it might upset our mother.

Parentheses lend a greater level of emphasis

> I'm afraid to go bungee jumping (though my brother tells me it's less frightening than a roller coaster).

Dashes indicate the highest level of emphasis and, sometimes, surprise and drama

> Christina felt as though she had been punched in the gut; she could hardly believe the stranger at her door was really who he claimed to be—the brother she hadn't seen in twenty years.

COMMON ERRORS

The art of typing a dash

Although dashes and hyphens may look similar, they are actually different marks. The distinction is small but important because dashes and hyphens serve different purposes. A dash is a line that is much longer than a hyphen. Most software will create a dash automatically when you type two hyphens together.

Do not leave a space between a dash or a hyphen and the words that come before and after them. Likewise, if you are using two hyphens to indicate a dash, do not leave a space between the hyphens.

(Continued on next page)

COMMON ERRORS *(Continued)*

Incorrect	A well - timed effort at conserving water may prevent long - term damage to drought - stricken farms - - if it's not already too late.
Correct	A well-timed effort at conserving water may prevent long-term damage to drought-stricken farms—if it's not already too late.

Remember: Do not put spaces before or after hyphens and dashes.

 31c Other Punctuation with Parentheses

Parentheses around letters or numbers that order a series within a sentence make the list easier to read.

> Angela Creider's recipe for becoming a great novelist is to (1) set aside an hour during the morning to write, (2) read what you've written out loud, (3) revise your prose, and (4) repeat this every morning for the next thirty years.

Abbreviations made from the first letters of words are often used in place of the unwieldy names of institutions, departments, organizations, or terms. To show readers what the abbreviation stands for, the writer must state the complete name, followed by the abbreviation in parentheses, the first time the organization is mentioned in the text.

> The University of California, Santa Cruz (UCSC) supports its mascot, the banana slug, with pride and a sense of humor. And although the nickname sounds strange to outsiders, UCSC students are even referred to as "the banana slugs."

COMMON ERRORS

Edit Help

Using periods, commas, colons, and semicolons with parentheses

When an entire sentence is enclosed in parentheses, place the period before the closing parenthesis.

Incorrect Our fear of sharks, heightened by movies like *Jaws*, is vastly out of proportion with the minor threat sharks actually pose. (Dying from a dog attack, in fact, is much more likely than dying from a shark attack).

Correct Our fear of sharks, heightened by movies like *Jaws*, is vastly out of proportion with the minor threat sharks actually pose. (Dying from a dog attack, in fact, is much more likely than dying from a shark attack.)

When the material in parentheses is part of the sentence and the parentheses fall at the end of the sentence, place the period outside the closing parenthesis.

Incorrect Reports of sharks attacking people are rare (much rarer than dog attacks.)

Correct Reports of sharks attacking people are rare (much rarer than dog attacks).

Place commas, colons, and semicolons after the closing parenthesis.

Remember: When an entire sentence is enclosed in parentheses, place the period inside the closing parenthesis; otherwise, put the punctuation outside the closing parenthesis.

32 Apostrophes

QUICK*TAKE*

- Use apostrophes to show possession (see below)
- Use apostrophes to show omitted letters (see p. 239)

32a Possessives

Nouns and indefinite pronouns (for example, *everyone, anyone*) that indicate possession or ownership are marked by attaching an apostrophe and *-s* or an apostrophe only to the end of the word.

Singular nouns and indefinite pronouns

For singular nouns and indefinite pronouns, add an apostrophe plus *-s: -'s*. Even singular nouns that end in *-s* usually follow this principle.

Iris's coat

everyone's favorite

a woman's choice

There are a few exceptions to adding *-'s* for singular nouns:

- **Awkward pronunciations** *Herodotus' travels, Jesus' sermons*
- **Official names of certain places, institutions, companies** *Governors Island, Teachers College of Columbia University, Mothers Café, Saks Fifth Avenue, Walgreens Pharmacy*. Note, however, that many companies do include the apostrophe: *Denny's Restaurant, Macy's, McDonald's, Wendy's Old Fashioned Hamburgers.*

Plural nouns

For plural nouns that do not end in *-s*, add an apostrophe plus *-s: -'s*.

media's responsibility

children's section

For plural nouns that end in *-s*, add only an apostrophe at the end.

attorneys' briefs

the Kennedys' legacy

Compound nouns

For compound nouns, add an apostrophe plus *-s* to the last word of the compound noun: *-'s*.

mayor of Cleveland's speech

Two or more nouns

For joint possession, add an apostrophe plus *-s* to the final noun: *-'s*.

mother and dad's yard

When people possess or own things separately, add an apostrophe plus *-s* to each noun: *-'s*.

Roberto's and Edward's views are totally opposed.

COMMON ERRORS

Possessive forms of personal pronouns never take the apostrophe

Incorrect *her's, it's, our's, your's, their's*

The bird sang in it's cage.

Correct *hers, its, ours, yours, theirs*

The bird sang in its cage.

Remember: *It's = It is*

32b Contractions and Omitted Letters

In speech we often leave out sounds and syllables of familiar words. These omissions are noted with apostrophes.

Contractions

Contractions combine two words into one, using the apostrophe to mark what is left out.

I am → I'm	we are → we're
you are → you're	they are → they're
you will → you'll	cannot → can't
he is → he's	do not → don't
she is → she's	does not → doesn't
it is → it's	will not → won't

Omissions

Using apostrophes to signal omitted letters is a way of approximating speech in writing. They can make your writing look informal and slangy, but overuse can quickly become annoying.

rock and roll → rock 'n' roll
neighborhood → 'hood

32c Plurals of Letters, Symbols, and Words Referred to as Words

When to use apostrophes to make plurals

The trend is away from using apostrophes to form plurals of letters, symbols, and words referred to as words. In a few cases, adding the apostrophe and *-s* is still used, as in this old saying:

Mind your p's and q's.

When not to use apostrophes to make plurals

Words used as words are italicized, and their plural is formed by adding an *-s* not in italics, not an apostrophe and *-s*.

Take a few of the *and*s out of your writing.

Do not use an apostrophe to make family names plural.

Incorrect	You've heard of keeping up with the Jones's.
Correct	You've heard of keeping up with the Joneses.

COMMON ERRORS

Do not use an apostrophe to make a noun plural

Incorrect The two government's agreed to meet.

Correct The two governments agreed to meet.

Remember: Add only *-s* = plural
Add apostrophe plus *-s* = possessive

33 Quotation Marks

QUICK*TAKE*

- Correctly incorporate words from quotations (see below)
- Use quotation marks correctly with other punctuation (see p. 243)

33a Direct Quotations

Use quotation marks to enclose direct quotations

Enclose direct quotations—someone else's words repeated verbatim—in quotation marks.

> Michael Pollan, the author of *Food Rule*s and *The Omnivore's Dilemma*, argues that industrial agriculture uses too much fossil fuel to grow food: "We need to reduce the dependence of modern agriculture on oil, an eminently feasible goal—after all, agriculture is the original solar technology."

Do not use quotation marks with indirect quotations

Do not enclose an indirect quotation—a paraphrase of someone else's words—in quotation marks. However, do remember that you need to cite your source not only when you quote directly but also when you paraphrase or borrow ideas.

> Dan Glickman of the Motion Picture Association of America (MPAA) thinks that because parents don't want their children to start smoking, they should be warned when movies contain scenes where characters smoke (98).

Do not use quotation marks with block quotations

When a quotation is long enough to be set off as a block quotation, do not use quotation marks. MLA style defines long quotations as more than four lines. APA style defines a long quotation as one that is more than forty words.

In the following example in MLA format, notice that the long quotation is indented and quotation marks are omitted. Also notice that the parenthetical citation for a long quotation comes after the period.

> Complaints about maintenance in the dorms have been on the rise ever since the physical plant reorganized its crews into teams in August. One student's experience is typical:
>
> > When our ceiling started dripping, my roommate and I went to our resident director right away to file an emergency maintenance request. By the fourth day without any word from a maintenance person, the ceiling tiles began to fall and puddles began to pool on our carpet. (Trillo)

 33b Titles of Short Works

While the titles of longer works such as books, magazines, and newspapers are italicized or underlined, titles of shorter works should be set off with quotation marks. Use quotation marks with the following kinds of titles.

Short stories	"Light Is Like Water" by Gabriel García Márquez
Magazine articles	"Race against Death" by Erin West

Newspaper articles	"Cincinnati Mayor Declares Emergency" by Liz Sidoti
Short poems	"We Real Cool" by Gwendolyn Brooks
Essays	"Self-Reliance" by Ralph Waldo Emerson

The exception. Don't put the title of your own paper in quotation marks. If the title of another short work appears within the title of your paper, retain the quotation marks around the short work.

33c Other Uses of Quotation Marks

Quotation marks around a term can indicate that the writer is using the term in a novel way, often with skepticism, irony, or sarcasm. The quotation marks indicate that the writer is questioning the term's conventional definition.

Italics are usually used to indicate that a word is being used as a word, rather than standing for its conventional meaning. However, quotation marks are correct in these cases as well.

> Beginning writers sometimes confuse "their," "they're," and "there."

33d Other Punctuation with Quotation Marks

The rules for placing punctuation with quotation marks fall into three general categories.

Periods and commas with quotation marks

Place periods and commas inside closing quotation marks.

Incorrect	"The smartest people", Dr. Geisler pointed out, "tell themselves the most convincing rationalizations".
Correct	"The smartest people," Dr. Geisler pointed out, "tell themselves the most convincing rationalizations."

Colons and semicolons with quotation marks

Place colons and semicolons outside closing quotation marks.

Incorrect "From Stettin in the Baltic to Trieste in the Adriatic, an iron curtain has descended across the Continent;" Churchill's statement rang through Cold War politics for the next fifty years.

Correct "From Stettin in the Baltic to Trieste in the Adriatic, an iron curtain has descended across the Continent"; Churchill's statement rang through Cold War politics for the next fifty years.

Exclamation points, question marks, and dashes with quotation marks

When an exclamation point, question mark, or dash belongs to the original quotation, place it inside the closing quotation mark. When it applies to the entire sentence, place it outside the closing quotation mark.

In the original quotation

"Are we there yet?" came the whine from the back seat.

Applied to the entire sentence

Did the driver in the front seat respond, "Not even close"?

COMMON ERRORS

e Edit Help

Quotations within quotations

Single quotation marks are used to indicate a quotation within a quotation. In the following example, single quotation marks clarify who is speaking. The rules for placing punctuation with single quotation marks are the same as the rules for placing punctuation with double quotation marks.

Incorrect When he showed the report to Paul Probius, Michener reported that Probius "took vigorous exception to the sentence "He wanted to close down the university," insisting that we add the clarifying phrase "as it then existed"" (Michener 145).

Correct When he showed the report to Paul Probius, Michener reported that Probius "took vigorous exception to the sentence 'He wanted to close down the university,' insisting that we add the clarifying phrase 'as it then existed'" (Michener 145).

Remember: Single quotation marks are used for quotations within quotations.

 Misuses of Quotation Marks

It's becoming more and more common to see quotation marks used to emphasize a word or phrase. Resist the temptation in your own writing; the usage is incorrect. In fact, because quotation marks indicate that a writer is using a term with skepticism or irony, adding quotation marks for emphasis will highlight unintended connotations of the term.

Incorrect "fresh" seafood

By using quotation marks here, the writer seems to call into question whether the seafood is really fresh.

Correct fresh seafood

Incorrect Enjoy our "live" music every Saturday night.

Again, the quotation marks unintentionally indicate that the writer is skeptical that the music is live.

Correct Enjoy our live music every Saturday night.

34 Other Punctuation Marks

QUICK*TAKE*

- Use periods, question marks, and exclamation points correctly (see below)
- Use brackets and ellipses correctly (see p. 249)

34a Periods

Periods at the ends of sentences

Place a period at the end of a complete sentence that is not a direct question or an exclamatory statement.

Periods with quotation marks and parentheses

When a quotation falls at the end of a sentence, place the period inside the closing quotation marks.

> Although he devoted decades to a wide range of artistic and political projects, Allen Ginsberg is best known as the author of the poem "Howl."

When a parenthetical phrase falls at the end of a sentence, place the period outside the closing parenthesis. When parentheses enclose a whole sentence, place the period inside the closing parenthesis.

Periods with abbreviations

Many abbreviations require periods; however, there are few set rules. The rules for punctuating two types of abbreviations do remain consistent: Postal abbreviations for states and most abbreviations for organizations do not require periods. When an abbreviation with a period falls at the end of a sentence, do not add a second period to conclude the sentence.

Incorrect	Her flight arrives at 6:22 p.m..
Correct	Her flight arrives at 6:22 p.m.

Periods as decimal points

Decimal points are periods that separate integers from tenths, hundredths, and so on.

99.98% pure silver — 98.6°F

on sale for $399.97 — 2.6-liter engine

34b Question Marks

Question marks with direct questions

Place a question mark at the end of a direct question. A direct question is one that the questioner puts to someone outright. In contrast, an indirect question merely reports the asking of a question. Question marks give readers a cue to read the end of the sentence with rising inflection. Read the following sentences aloud. Hear how your inflection rises in the second sentence to convey the direct question.

Indirect question

Desirée asked whether Dan rides his motorcycle without a helmet.

Direct question

Desirée asked, "Does Dan ride his motorcycle without a helmet?"

Question marks with quotations

When a quotation falls at the end of a direct question, place the question mark outside the closing quotation mark.

> Did Abraham Lincoln really call Harriet Beecher Stowe "the little lady who started this big war"?

Place the question mark inside the closing quotation when only the quoted material is a direct question.

> Slowly scientists are beginning to answer the question "Is cancer a genetic disease?"

When quoting a direct question in the middle of a sentence, place a question mark inside the closing quotation mark and place a period at the end of the sentence.

> Market researchers estimate that asking Burger World's customers "Do you want fries with that?" was responsible for a 15% boost in french fries sales.

 Exclamation Points

Exclamation points to convey strong emotion

Exclamation points conclude sentences and, like question marks, tell the reader how a sentence should sound. They indicate strong emotion. Use exclamation points sparingly in formal writing; they are seldom appropriate in academic and professional prose.

Exclamation points with emphatic interjections

Exclamation points can convey a sense of urgency with brief interjections. Interjections can be incorporated into sentences or stand on their own.

> Run! They're about to close the doors to the jetway.

Exclamation points with quotation marks

In quotations, exclamation points follow the same rules as question marks. If a quotation falls at the end of an exclamatory statement, place the exclamation point outside the closing quotation mark.

> The singer forgot the words to "America the Beautiful"!

When quoting an exclamatory statement at the end of a sentence that is not itself exclamatory, place the exclamation point inside the closing quotation mark.

> Jerry thought his car would be washed away in the flood, but Anna jumped into action, declaring, "Not if I can help it!"

34d Brackets

While brackets (sometimes called *square brackets*) look quite similar to parentheses, the two perform different functions. Brackets have a narrow set of uses.

Brackets to provide clarification within quotation marks

Use brackets if you are interjecting a comment of your own or clarifying information within a direct quotation. In the following example, the writer quotes a sentence with the pronoun *they,* which refers to a noun in a previous, unquoted sentence. The material in brackets clarifies to whom the pronoun refers.

> The Harris study found that "In the last three years, they [Gonzales Junior High students] averaged 15% higher on their mathematics assessment tests than their peers in Northridge County."

Brackets within parentheses

Since parentheses within parentheses might confuse readers, use brackets to enclose parenthetical information within a parenthetical phrase.

> Representative Patel's most controversial legislation (including a version of the hate crimes bill [HR 99-108] the house rejected two years ago) has a slim chance of being enacted this session.

34e Ellipses

Ellipses let a reader know that a portion of a passage is missing. You can use ellipses to keep quotations concise and direct readers' attention to what is important about the point you are making. An ellipsis is a string of three periods with spaces separating the periods.

Ellipses to indicate an omission from a quotation

When you quote only a phrase or a short clause from a sentence, you usually do not need to use an ellipsis.

> Mao Zedong first used "let a hundred flowers blossom" in a Beijing speech in 1957.

Except at the beginning of a quotation, indicate omitted words with an ellipsis.

> "The female praying mantis . . . tears off her male partner's head during mating."

When the ellipsis is at the end of a sentence, place the period or question mark after the ellipsis and follow with the closing quotation mark.

Words omitted at the end of a sentence

> "This brutal dance is a stark example of the innate evolutionary drive to pass genes onto offspring. . . ."

35 Capitalization, Italics, Abbreviations, and Numbers

QUICK*TAKE*

- Capitalize words properly (see below)
- Use italics correctly (see p. 251)
- Use abbreviations correctly (see p. 251)

35a Capital Letters

Capitalize the initial letters of proper nouns (nouns that name particular people, places, and things). Capitalize the initial letters of proper adjectives (adjectives based on the names of people, places, and things).

African American bookstore   Avogadro's number   Irish music

Do not capitalize the names of seasons, academic disciplines (unless they are languages), or job titles used without a proper noun.

35b Italics

Italicize the titles of entire works (books, magazines, newspapers, films), but place the titles of parts of those works within quotation marks. Also italicize or underline the names of ships and aircraft.

> I am fond of reading *USA Today* in the morning.

The exceptions. Do not italicize or underline the names of sacred texts.

Italicize unfamiliar foreign words

Italicize foreign words that are not part of common English usage. Do not italicize words that have become a common word or phrase in the English vocabulary. How do you decide which words are common? If a word appears in a standard English dictionary, it can be considered as adopted into English.

Use italics to clarify your use of a word, letter, or number

In everyday speech, we often use cues—a pause, a louder or different tone—to communicate how we are using a word. In writing, italics help clarify when you use words in a referential manner, or letters and numbers as letters and numbers.

35c Abbreviations

Abbreviations are shortened forms of words. Because abbreviations vary widely, you will need to look in the dictionary to determine how to abbreviate words on a case-by-case basis. Nonetheless, there are a few patterns that abbreviations follow.

Abbreviate titles before and degrees after full names

> Ms. Ella Fitzgerald
>
> Prof. Vijay Aggarwal

Write out the professional title when it is used with only a last name.

Professor Chin

Reverend Ames

Conventions for using abbreviations with years and times

BCE (before the common era) and CE (common era) are now preferred for indicating years, replacing BC (before Christ) and AD (*anno Domini* ["the year of our Lord"]). Note that all are now used without periods.

479 **BCE** (or BC)

1610 **CE** (or AD, but AD would be placed before the number)

The preferred written conventions for times are a.m. (*ante meridiem*) and p.m. (*post meridiem*).

9:03 **a.m.**

3:30 **p.m.**

Latin abbreviations

Some writers sprinkle Latin abbreviations throughout their writing, apparently thinking that they are a mark of learning. Frequently these abbreviations are used inappropriately. If you use Latin abbreviations, make sure you know what they stand for.

e.g. (*exempli gratia*) for example

et al. (*et alia*) and others

etc. (*et cetera*) and so forth

i.e. (*id est*) that is

N.B. (*nota bene*) note well

In particular, avoid using *etc.* to fill out a list of items. Use of *etc.* announces that you haven't taken the time to finish a thought.

Lazy The contents of his grocery cart described his eating habits: a big bag of chips, hot sauce, frozen pizza, **etc.**

Better The contents of his grocery cart described his eating habits: a big bag of chips, a large jar of hot sauce, two frozen pizzas, a twelve-pack of cola, three Mars bars, and a package of Twinkies.

Conventions for using abbreviations in formal writing

Most abbreviations are inappropriate in formal writing except when the reader would be more familiar with the abbreviation than with the words it represents. When your reader is unlikely to be familiar with an abbreviation, spell out the term, followed by the abbreviation in parentheses, the first time you use it in a paper. The reader will then understand what the abbreviation refers to, and you may use the abbreviation in subsequent sentences.

> The **Office of Civil Rights (OCR)** is the agency that enforces Title IX regulations. In 1979 **OCR** set out three options for schools to comply with Title IX.

35d Acronyms

Acronyms are abbreviations formed from the first letter of each word. Acronyms are pronounced as words.

AIDS for Acquired Immunodeficiency Syndrome

NASA for National Air and Space Administration

Initial-letter abbreviations are commonly pronounced as letters.

ACLU for American Civil Liberties Union

HIV for human immunodeficiency virus

rpm for revolutions per minute

Familiar acronyms and initial-letter abbreviations, such as CBS, CIA, FBI, IQ, and UN, are rarely spelled out. Unfamiliar acronyms and abbreviations should always be spelled out. Acronyms and abbreviations that frequently are used in particular fields should be spelled out on first use. For example, MMPI (Minnesota Multiphasic Personality Inventory) is a familiar abbreviation in psychology but will be unfamiliar to those outside that discipline.

 Numbers

In formal writing spell out any number that can be expressed in one or two words, as well as any number, regardless of length, at the beginning of a sentence. Also, hyphenate two-word numbers from twenty-one to ninety-nine. When a sentence begins with a number that requires more than two words, revise it if possible.

The exceptions. Most scientific reports and some business writing use numerals consistently. Most styles do not write out in words a year, a date, an address, a page number, the time of day, decimals, sums of money, phone numbers, rates of speed, or the scene and act of a play. Use numerals instead.

> In **2001** only **33%** of respondents said they were satisfied with the City Council's proposals to help the homeless.
>
> The **17** trials were conducted at temperatures of **12–14°C** with results ranging from **2.43** to **2.89** mg/dl.

When one number modifies another number, write one out and express the other in numeral form.

> In the last year, all **four 8th** Street restaurants began to donate their leftovers to the soup kitchen.
>
> Only after Meryl had run in **12 fifty**-mile ultramarathons did she finally win first place in her age group.

Glossary of Grammatical Terms and Usage

The glossary gives the definitions of grammatical terms and items of usage. The grammatical terms are shown in **blue**. Some of the explanations of usage that follow are not rules, but guidelines to keep in mind for academic and professional writing. In these formal contexts, the safest course is to avoid words that are described as *nonstandard, informal,* or *colloquial.*

a/an Use *a* before words that begin with a consonant sound (*a train, a house*). Use *an* before words that begin with a vowel sound (*an airplane, an hour*).

a lot/alot *A lot* is generally regarded as informal; *alot* is nonstandard.

accept/except *Accept* is a verb meaning "receive" or "approve." *Except* is sometimes a verb meaning "leave out," but much more often it's used as a conjunction or preposition meaning "other than."

active A clause with a transitive verb in which the subject is the doer of the action (see Section 18a). See also **passive.**

adjective A modifier that qualifies or describes the qualities of a noun or pronoun (see Sections 27a and 27b).

adjective clause A subordinate clause that modifies a noun or pronoun and is usually introduced by a relative pronoun (see Section 27b). Sometimes called a *relative clause.*

adverb A word that modifies a verb, another modifier, or a clause (see Sections 27a and 27c).

adverb clause A subordinate clause that functions as an adverb by modifying a verb, another modifier, or a clause (see Section 27c).

advice/advise The noun *advice* means a "suggestion"; the verb *advise* means to "recommend" or "give advice."

affect/effect Usually, *affect* is a verb (to "influence") and *effect* is a noun (a "result"). Less commonly, *affect* is used as a noun and *effect* as a verb.

agreement The number and person of a subject and verb must match—singular subjects with singular verbs, plural subjects with plural verbs (see Chapter 23). Likewise, the number and gender of a pronoun and its antecedent must match (see Section 25b).

all ready/already The adjective phrase *all ready* means "completely prepared"; the adverb *already* means "previously."

all right/alright *All right,* meaning "acceptable," is the correct spelling. *Alright* is nonstandard.

allude/elude *Allude* means "refer to indirectly." *Elude* means "evade."

allusion/illusion An *allusion* is an indirect reference; an *illusion* is a false impression.

among/between *Between* refers to precisely two people or things; *among refers* to three or more.

amount/number Use *amount* with things that cannot be counted; use *number* with things that can be counted.

an See **a/an.**

antecedent The noun (or pronoun) that a pronoun refers to (see Section 25b).

anybody/any body; anyone/any one *Anybody* and *anyone* are indefinite pronouns and have the same meaning. In *any body, body* is a noun modified by *any,* and in *any one, one* is a pronoun or adjective modified by *any.*

anymore/any more *Anymore* means "now," while *any more* means "no more." Both are used in negative constructions.

anyway/anyways *Anyway* is correct. *Anyways* is nonstandard.

articles The words *a, an,* and *the* (see Section 28b).

as/as if/as though/like Use *as* instead of *like* before dependent clauses (which include a subject and verb). Use *like* before a noun or a pronoun.

assure/ensure/insure *Assure* means "promise," *ensure* means "make certain," and *insure* means to "make certain in either a legal or financial sense."

auxiliary verb Forms of *be, do,* and *have* combine with verbs to indicate tense and mood (see Section 28c). The modal verbs *can, could, may, might, must, shall, should, will,* and *would* are a subset of auxiliaries.

bad/badly Use *bad* only as an adjective. *Badly* is the adverb.

being as/being that Both constructions are colloquial and awkward substitutes for *because.* Don't use them in formal writing.

beside/besides *Beside* means "next to." *Besides* means "in addition to" or "except."

between See **among/between.**

bring/take *Bring* describes movement from a more distant location to a nearer one. *Take* describes movement away.

can/may In formal writing, *can* indicates ability or capacity, while *may* indicates permission.

case The form of a noun or pronoun that indicates its function. Nouns change case only to show possession: the *dog,* the *dog's* bowl. See **pronoun case** (Section 25a).

censor/censure To *censor* is to edit or ban on moral or political grounds. To *censure* is to reprimand publicly.

cite/sight/site To *cite* is to "mention specifically"; *sight as* a verb means to "observe" and as a noun refers to "vision"; *site* is most commonly used as a noun that means "location," but it is also used as a verb to mean "situate."

clause A group of words with a subject and a predicate. A main or independent clause can stand as a sentence. A subordinate or dependent clause must be attached to a main clause to form a sentence (see Section 22a).

collective noun A noun that refers to a group or a plurality, such as *team, army,* or *committee* (see Section 23d).

comma splice Two independent clauses joined incorrectly by a comma (see Section 22c).

common noun A noun that names a general group, person, place, or thing (see Section 28a). Common nouns are not capitalized unless they begin a sentence.

complement A word or group of words that completes the predicate. See also **linking verb.**

complement/compliment To *complement* something is to complete it or make it perfect; to *compliment* is to flatter.

complex sentence A sentence that contains at least one subordinate clause attached to a main clause.

compound sentence A sentence that contains at least two main clauses.

compound-complex sentence A sentence that contains at least two main clauses and one subordinate clause.

conjunction See **coordinating conjunction** and **subordinating conjunction.**

conjunctive adverb An adverb that often modifies entire clauses and sentences, such as *also, consequently, however, indeed, instead, moreover, nevertheless, otherwise, similarly,* and *therefore* (see Section 27c).

continual/continuous *Continual* refers to a repeated activity; *continuous* refers to an ongoing, unceasing activity.

coordinate A relationship of equal importance, in terms of either grammar or meaning (see Section 20c).

coordinating conjunction A word that links two equivalent grammatical elements, such as *and, but, or, yet, nor, for,* and *so.*

could of Nonstandard. See **have/of.**

count noun A noun that names things that can be counted, such as *block, cat,* and *toy* (see Section 28a).

cumulative adjective Two or more adjectives not separated by a comma because they do not make sense if the order is changed. For example, an *enormous dump truck* cannot be changed to a *dump enormous truck* (see Section 29e).

dangling modifier A modifier that is not clearly attached to what it modifies (see Section 27e).

data The plural form of *datum;* it takes plural verb forms.

declarative A sentence that makes a statement.

dependent clause See **subordinate clause**.

determiners Words that initiate noun phrases, including possessive nouns (*Pedro's*); possessive pronouns (*my, your*); demonstrative pronouns (*this, that*); and indefinite pronouns (*all, both, many*).

differ from/differ with To *differ from* means to "be unlike"; to *differ with* means to "disagree."

different from/different than Use *different from* where possible.

*Dark French roast is **different from** ordinary coffee.*

direct object A noun, pronoun, or noun clause that names who or what receives the action of a transitive verb.

discreet/discrete Both are adjectives. *Discreet* means "prudent" or "tactful"; *discrete* means "separate."

disinterested/uninterested *Disinterested* is often misused to mean *uninterested.* Disinterested means "impartial." A judge can be interested in a case but disinterested in the outcome.

double negative The incorrect use of two negatives to signal the same negative meaning.

due to the fact that Avoid this wordy substitute for *because.*

each other/one another Use *each other* for two; use *one another* for more than two.

effect See **affect/effect.**

elicit/illicit The verb *elicit* means to "draw out." The adjective *illicit* means "unlawful."

emigrate from/immigrate to *Emigrate* means to "leave one's country"; *immigrate to* means to "settle in another country."

ensure See **assure/ensure/insure.**

enthused Nonstandard in academic and professional writing. Use *enthusiastic* instead.

etc. Avoid this abbreviation for the Latin *et cetera* in formal writing. Either list all the items or use an English phrase such as *and so forth.*

every body/everybody; every one/everyone *Everybody* and *everyone* are indefinite pronouns referring to all people under discussion. *Every one* and *every body* are adjective-noun combinations referring to all members of a group.

except See **accept/except.**

except for the fact that Avoid this wordy substitute for *except that.*

expletive The dummy subjects *it* and *there* used to fill a grammatical slot in a sentence.

It is raining outside. There should be a law against it.

explicit/implicit Both are adjectives; *explicit* means "stated outright," while *implicit* means just the opposite, "unstated."

farther/further *Farther* refers to physical distance; *further* refers to time or other abstract concepts.

fewer/less Use *fewer* with what can be counted and *less* with what cannot be counted.

flunk In formal writing, avoid this colloquial substitute for *fail.*

fragment A group of words beginning with a capital letter and ending with a period that looks like a sentence but lacks a subject or a predicate or both (see Section 22a).

further See **farther/further.**

gerund An *-ing* form of a verb used as a noun, such as *running, skiing,* or *laughing.*

good/well *Good* is an adjective and is not interchangeable with the adverb *well.* The one exception is health. Both she feels *good* and she feels *well* are correct.

hanged/hung Use *hanged* to refer only to executions; *hung* is used for all other instances.

have/of *Have,* not *of,* follows *should, could, would, may, must,* and *might.*

he/she; s/he Try to avoid language that appears to exclude either gender (unless this is intended, of course) and awkward compromises such as *he/she* or *s/he.* The best solution is to make pronouns plural (the gender-neutral *they*) wherever possible (see Section 25c).

helping verb See **auxiliary verb**.

hopefully This adverb is commonly used as a sentence modifier, but many readers object to it.

illusion See **allusion/illusion.**

immigrate See **emigrate from/immigrate to.**

imperative A sentence that expresses a command. Usually, the subject is implied rather than stated.

implicit See **explicit/implicit.**

imply/infer *Imply* means to "suggest"; *infer* means to "draw a conclusion."

in regards to Avoid this wordy substitute for *regarding.*

incredible/incredulous *Incredible* means "unbelievable"; *incredulous* means "not believing."

independent clause See **main clause.**

indirect object A noun, pronoun, or noun clause that names who or what is affected by the action of a transitive verb.

infinitive The word *to* plus the base verb form: *to believe, to feel, to act.* See also **split infinitive.**

infinitive phrase A phrase that uses the infinitive form of a verb.

interjection A word expressing feeling that is grammatically unconnected to a sentence, such as *cool, wow, ouch,* or *yikes.*

interrogative A sentence that asks a question.

intransitive verb A verb that does not take an object, such as *sleep, appear,* or *laugh* (see Sections 24c and 28c).

irregardless Nonstandard for *regardless.*

irregular verb A verb that does not use either *-d* or *-ed* to form the past tense and past participle (see Section 24b).

it is my opinion that Avoid this wordy substitute for *I believe that.*

its/it's *Its* is the possessive of *it* and does not take an apostrophe; *it's* is the contraction for *it is.*

-ize/-wise The suffix *-ize* changes a noun or adjective into a verb (*harmony, harmonize*). The suffix *-wise* changes a noun or adjective into an adverb (*clock, clockwise*). Some writers are tempted to use these suffixes to convert almost any word into an adverb or verb form. Unless the word appears in a dictionary, don't use it.

kind of/sort of/type of Avoid using these colloquial expressions if you mean *somewhat* or *rather. It's kind of hot* is nonstandard. Each is permissible, however, when it refers to a classification of an object. Be sure that it agrees in number with the object it is modifying.

lay/lie *Lay* means "place" or "put" and generally takes a direct object (see Section 24c). Its main forms are *lay, laid, laid. Lie* means "recline" or "be positioned" and does not take an object. Its main forms are *lie, lay, lain.*

less See **fewer/less.**

lie See **lay/lie.**

linking verb A verb that connects the subject to the complement, such as *appear, be, feel, look, seem,* or *taste.*

lots/lots of Nonstandard in formal writing; use *many* or *much* instead.

main clause A group of words with a subject and a predicate that can stand alone as a sentence. Also called an *independent clause.*

mankind This term offends some readers and is outdated. Use *humans, humanity,* or *people* instead.

may/can See **can/may.**

may be/maybe *May be* is a verb phrase; *maybe* is an adverb.

media This is the plural form of the noun *medium* and requires a plural verb.

might of See **have/of.**

modal A kind of auxiliary verb that indicates ability, permission, intention, obligation, or probability, such as *can, could, may, might, must, shall, should, will,* or *would.*

modifier A general term for adjectives, adverbs, phrases, and clauses that describe other words (see Chapter 27).

must of See **have/of.**

noncount noun A noun that names things that cannot be counted, such as *air, energy,* or *water* (see Section 28a).

nonrestrictive modifier A modifier that is not essential to the meaning of the word, phrase, or clause it modifies and should be set off by commas or other punctuation (see Section 29c).

noun The name of a person, place, thing, concept, or action. See also **common noun** and **proper noun** (see Section 28a).

noun clause A subordinate clause that functions as a noun.

number See **amount/number.**

object Receiver of the action within the clause or phrase.

OK, O.K., okay Informal; avoid using in academic and professional writing. Each spelling is accepted in informal usage.

owing to the fact that Avoid this wordy, colloquial substitute for *because.*

parallelism The principle of putting similar elements or ideas in similar grammatical form (see Section 20c).

participle A form of a verb that uses *-ing* in the present (*laughing, playing*) and usually *-ed* or *-en* in the past (*laughed, played*). See Section 24a. Participles are either part of the verb phrase (*She had played the game before*) or used as adjectives (*the laughing girl*).

participial phrase A phrase formed either by a present participle (for example, *racing*) or by a past participle (for example, *taken*).

parts of speech The eight classes of words according to their grammatical function: nouns, pronouns, verbs, adjectives, adverbs, prepositions, conjunctions, and interjections.

passive A clause with a transitive verb in which the subject is being acted upon (see Section 18a). See also **active.**

people/persons *People* refers to a general group; *persons* refers to a collection of individuals. Use *people* over *persons* except when you're emphasizing the idea of separate persons within the group.

per Try not to use the English equivalent of this Latin word except in technical writing or familiar usages like *miles per gallon.*

phenomena This is the plural form of *phenomenon* ("observable fact" or "unusual event") and takes a plural verb.

phrase A group of words that does not contain both a subject and predicate.

plenty In academic and professional writing, avoid this colloquial substitute for *very.*

plus Do not use *plus* to join clauses or sentences. Use *and, also, moreover, furthermore,* or another conjunctive adverb instead.

precede/proceed Both are verbs, but they have different meanings: *precede* means "come before," and *proceed* means "go ahead" or "continue."

predicate The part of the clause that expresses the action or tells something about the subject. The predicate includes the verb and all its complements, objects, and modifiers.

prejudice/prejudiced *Prejudice* is a noun; *prejudiced* is an adjective.

preposition A class of words that indicate relationships and qualities.

prepositional phrase A phrase formed by a preposition and its object, including the modifiers of its object.

principal/principle *Principal* means first in importance (*school principal, principal reason*). *Principle* applies to beliefs or understandings (*It goes against my principles*).

pronoun A word that stands for other nouns or pronouns. Pronouns have several subclasses, including personal pronouns, possessive pronouns, demonstrative pronouns, indefinite pronouns, relative pronouns, interrogative pronouns, reflexive pronouns, and reciprocal pronouns (Chapter 25).

pronoun case Pronouns that function as the subjects of sentences are in the **subjective** case (*I, you, he, she, it, we, they*). Pronouns that function as direct or indirect objects are in the **objective** case (*me, you, him, her, it, us, them*). Pronouns that indicate ownership are in the **possessive** case (*my, your, his, her, its, our, their*) (see Section 25a).

proper noun A noun that names a particular person, place, thing, or group (see Section 28a). Proper nouns are capitalized.

question as to whether/question of whether Avoid these wordy substitutes for *whether.*

raise/rise The verb *raise* means "lift up" and takes a direct object. Its main forms are *raise, raised, raised.* The verb *rise* means "get up" and does not take a direct object. Its main forms are *rise, rose, risen.*

real/really Avoid using *real* as if it were an adverb. *Really* is an adverb; *real* is an adjective.

reason is because Omit either *reason is* or *because* when explaining causality.

reason why Avoid using this redundant combination.

relative pronoun A pronoun that initiates clauses, such as *that, which, what, who, whom,* or *whose.*

restrictive modifier A modifier that is essential to the meaning of the word, phrase, or clause it modifies (see Section 29c). Restrictive modifiers are usually not set off by punctuation.

rise/raise See **raise/rise.**

run-on sentence Two main clauses fused together without punctuation or a conjunction, appearing as one sentence (see Section 22b).

sentence A grammatically independent group of words that contains at least one main clause.

sentence fragment See **fragment**.

set/sit Set means "put" and takes a direct object; its main forms are *set, set, set. Sit* means "be seated" and does not take a direct object; its main forms are *sit, sat, sat. Sit* should not be used as a synonym for *set.*

shall/will *Shall* is used most often in first person questions, while *will* is a future tense helping verb for all persons. British English consistently uses *shall* with first person: *I shall, we shall.*

should of See **have/of.**

sit/set See **set/sit.**

some time/sometime/sometimes *Some time* means "a span of time," *sometime* means "at some unspecified time," and *sometimes* means "occasionally."

somebody/some body; someone/some one *Somebody* and *someone* are indefinite pronouns and have the same meaning. In *some body, body* is a noun modified by *some,* and in *some one, one* is a pronoun or adjective modified by *some.*

sort of See **kind of/sort of/type of.**

split infinitive An infinitive with a word or words between *to* and the base verb form, such as *to boldly go, to better appreciate.*

stationary/stationery *Stationary* means "motionless"; *stationery* means "writing paper."

subject A noun, pronoun, or noun phrase that identifies what the clause is about and connects with the predicate.

subject-verb agreement See **agreement**.

subordinate A relationship of unequal importance, in terms of either grammar or meaning (see Section 20a).

subordinate clause A clause that cannot stand alone but must be attached to a main clause. Also called a *dependent clause.*

subordinating conjunction A word that introduces a subordinate clause. Common subordinating conjunctions are *after, although, as, because, before, if, since, that, unless, until, when, where,* and *while.*

sure A colloquial term used as an adverb to mean "certainly." Avoid using it this way in formal writing.

sure and/sure to; try and/try to *Sure to* and *try to* are correct; do not use *and* after *sure* or *try.*

take See **bring/take.**

that/which *That* introduces a restrictive or essential clause. Restrictive clauses describe an object that must be that particular object and no other. Though some writers occasionally use *which* with restrictive clauses, *which* is most often used to introduce nonrestrictive clauses. These are clauses that contain additional nonessential information about the object (see Section 29c).

transition A word or phrase that notes movement from one unit of writing to another.

transitive verb A verb that takes a direct object (see Section 24c).

unique *Unique* means one of a kind. Things cannot be "very unique" or "more unique." They are either unique or not.

verb A word that expresses action or characterizes the subject in some way. Verbs can show tense and mood (see Chapter 24 and Section 28c).

verbal A form of a verb used as an adjective, adverb, or noun. See also **gerund, infinitive, participle.**

well/good See **good/well.**

which/that See **that/which.**

who/whom *Who* and *whom* follow the same rules as other pronouns: *Who* is the subject pronoun; *whom* is the object pronoun (see Section 25a).

will/shall See **shall/will.**

-wise/-ize See **-ize/-wise.**

would of See **have/of.**

you Avoid indefinite uses of *you. You* should only be used to mean "you, the reader."

your/you're The two are not interchangeable. *Your* is the possessive form of *you; you're* is the contraction of *you are.*

Index

A

D

E

F

G

H

I

J

K

L

O

P

T

Credits

p. 6: Library of Congress Prints and Photographs Division, Dorothea Lange/Farm Security Administration/Office of War Information Black-and-White Negatives [LC-DIG-fsa-8b31801].

p. 65: Excerpt from *Walkable City: How Downtown Can Save America, One Step at a Time* by Jeff Speck. Copyright © 2012 by Jeff Speck. Reproduced by permission of Farrar, Straus and Giroux, LLC.

p. 70: Rozin, Paul, Rebecca Bauer, and Dana Catanese, "Food and Life, Pleasure and Worry, Among American College Students: Gender Differences and Regional Similarities." *Journal of Psychology and Social Psychology* 85.1 (2003): 132. PsycARTICLES. Web. 6 Apr. 2013.

p. 72: Screenshot, EBSCO database search results screen from EBSCOhost. Copyright © EBSCO Information Services. All rights reserved. Reproduced by permission of EBSCO Publishing.

p. 78: Pilgram, Sarah, David Smith, and Jules Pretty, "A Cross-Regional Assessment of the Factors Affecting Ecoliteracy: Implications for Policy and Practice." *Ecological Applications* 17.6 (2007): 1742-51.

p. 80: Book cover of *In Defense of Food: An Eater's Manifesto* by Michael Pollan. Penguin Press.

p. 82: EBSCOhost screenshot with an excerpt from *Occupational Outlook Quarterly* from EBSCOhost. Copyright © EBSCO Information Services. All rights reserved. Reproduced by permission of EBSCO Publishing.

p. 84: Screenshot, *Colby Magazine* from Colby College. Reproduced by permission of Colby College.

p. 120: Linda Resnik, Melissa Gray, Matthew Borgia, *Journal of Rehabilitation Research and Development.* United States Department of Veterans Affairs, Vol 48, Number 2, 2011, pages 89–102.

p. 122: Title page for *Five Minds for the Future* by Howard Gardner, 2007. Reproduced by permission of Harvard Business School Press.

p. 124: Screenshot, Environmental Health Perspectives Web page from Environmental Health Perspectives (2005). Reproduced with permission from Environmental Health Perspectives.

Unless otherwise noted, all text, photos, and illustrations © Lester Faigley.

REVISION GUIDE

Commonly used editing and proofreading symbols are listed here, along with references to the relevant chapters and sections of this handbook.

Words, Sentences, and Paragraphs

abbr	Abbreviation problem: 35c
adj	Adjective problem: 27a-b
adv	Adverb problem: 27a, 27c
agr	Agreement problem, either subject-verb or pronoun-antecedent: 23, 25b
apos	Apostrophe missing or misused: 32
art	Article is missing or misused: 28b
cap	Capitalization is needed: 35a
case	Case of a pronoun is incorrect: 25a
coh	Coherence lacking in a paragraph: 3d
cs	Comma splice occurs: 22c
dm	Dangling modifier appears: 27e
frag	Fragment instead of complete sentence: 22a
ital	Italics missing or misused: 35b
lc	Lower case needed: 35a
mm	Misplaced modifier: 27b-c
num	Number problem: 35e
p	Punctuation problem: 29-34
pass	Passive voice misused: 18a
pl	Plural form misused or needed: 28a
pron	Pronoun problem: 25
ref	Reference of a pronoun unclear: 25d
run-on	Run-on sentence problem: 22b
sexist	Sexist language: 21d
sp	Spelling needs to be checked: 4d
sub	Subordination is faulty: 20a
trans	Transition misused or needed: 4c
vb	Verb problem: 24
w	Wordy: 19
ww	Wrong word: 21
¶	Paragraph break needed: 3
no ¶	No paragraph break needed: 3
//	Parallelism needs to be checked: 20c

Punctuation and Mechanics

^,	Comma needed: 29
'	Apostrophe needed: 32
" "	Quotation marks needed: 33
⊙	Period needed: 34a
?	Question mark needed: 34b
!	Exclamation point needed: 34c
—	Dash needed: 31
. . .	Ellipses needed: 34e
( )	Parentheses needed: 31
[ ]	Brackets needed: 34d
#	Add a space
⁀	Close up a space
⌇	Delete this
^	Insert something
∽	Transpose (switch the order)

Contents

PART 1 Composing

PART 2 Planning Research and Finding Sources

PART 3 Incorporating and Documenting Sources